DO

道

THE PATH OF CONTINUOUS GROWTH

GENARO TORRES CELIS

Praise for *Do*

"In this book, Genaro has taken a lifetime of practicing a variety of Japanese martial arts—not in just the physical aspect, but in the psychological, emotional, and spiritual aspects—and blended them with his many years of business consulting and executive coaching. And it's a powerful blend!

Beginning with personal stories of finding ever-deeper meaning and growth in his martial-arts practices (from which we can gain insights into our own life trajectories), he then shows us how to apply the principles in a highly practical, real-world, and relevant way through the Personal Strategy Canvas™—an approach to life and career design he created and has used as a tool for his clients for many years now.

The combination of ancient Japanese wisdom and modern-day business and executive coaching is unexpected, unusual, and effective. Whether you're pursuing personal goals, a professional career, or leading a business, his approach is widely applicable and valuable."

—Grace Judson, author of *The Five Deadly Shoulds of Office Politics: How they mangle your career (and what to do about them)*

"*Do: The Path of Continuous Growth* gives you possibilities that can help you grow both personally and professionally. Genaro guides you to take action by creating your Personal Strategy Canvas™. A must-read for anyone who continues to seek self-development."

—Annella Metoyer, author of *Dare to Be the Change* and *Stronger than Fear*

"Creating an organizational culture that serves both the people and the organization starts with developing the leaders in the organization. Through years of work, first on his own growth and then serving leaders around the world on their journeys, Genaro Torres has developed a powerful process. While the depth of reflection and effort required for true personal growth and development mean this book is for the courageous, the process itself is clear and simple. When you are ready to invest the time and energy in being your best self, this is your go-to resource."

—Cathy Liska, MCC and CEO of the Center for Coaching Certification

"Reading *Do: The Path of Continuous Growth* is like sitting with your best friend having coffee or wine— the conversation just flows. It's that juicy, candid, and honest conversation that does not want to end. With the right amounts of deep, thought provoking philosophy and solid practical application, this book takes us on a powerful journey of discovery, introspection, and realization. A call for action and decision, *Do* is truly a foundational read for those embarking on the path of leadership, and real inspiration and transformation for those already on it."

—Gaby Alvarez-Pollack, CLO and founder of GS&L Consulting

"A delightful guide full of important and extremely practical information for those who want to enjoy the path of leadership through the positive impact on others—definitively a life changing book."

—Jose Moreno, founder and CEO of MBGE Intersystems

"Agile, interesting, fun, educating, and easy to read, yet very deep in thoughts and insights. An excellent reference and practical guide to transform your business or every aspect of your personal life. In this book, Genaro reflects on the congruency and consistency with which he 'walks the walk' in his trainings, seminars, coaching sessions, and day-to-day life."

—Gustavo Guerra, Americas PMO Manager at HP Inc.

"This book is both a memoir and a guide to living your best life, and I could feel Genaro's authenticity pouring through the pages. He pulls inspiration from his extensive experience in martial arts, business, and coaching, to walk you through a journey of self-discovery and self-expression."

—Tom Thompson, consultant and curriculum development manager at WECA

"The most difficult part of any journey is knowing how to start. In *Do*, author Genaro Torres charts a clear path for becoming your best self, both personally and professionally. He draws upon wisdom from his lifelong experience in both martial arts and business to lay out step-by-step guidance to fulfilling your dreams."

—Jeff Toister, author of *Getting Service Right*, *The Service Culture Handbook*, and *Customer Service Tip of the Week*

Do

DO

道

THE PATH OF CONTINUOUS GROWTH

GENARO TORRES CELIS

Dedication

For my family, my friends, and people who make their dreams come true.

Nothing is impossible to a willing mind.

—Books of Han Dynasty

Table of Contents

Foreword

How often do people meander through life to accidentally end up where they end up? It seems more often than makes sense. What is the alternative? Awareness, choice, and action. Of course, the challenge is the starting point: awareness. The awareness that there are options. Recognizing that whether the past was traumatic or ideal, the future remains a choice. Awareness that creating the desired future requires learning, choosing, and acting. In this book, Genaro captures the essence of this reality and provides a door through awareness.

Early in 2010 I had the privilege of getting to know Genaro while he completed a coaching certification. When he reached out again seven years later, after I'd certified hundreds of other students, I remembered exactly who he was—after all, I had been sharing something he said with other students all along. Genaro had pointed out the difference between asking, "How can we be the best *of* the world?" and "How can we be the best *for* the world?"

Throughout his coaching certification, I had been aware of his undercurrent of strength and integrity. Genaro referenced martial arts, which I knew he was heavily involved in. Because martial arts were something of which my knowledge was limited, my awareness was also limited. Now, through this book, the wisdom that comes from martial arts is accessible for all who dare to expand and challenge their thinking while progressing on the journey to be their best self.

Genaro openly shares his personal experiences, challenges, and insights. With his authentic vulnerability and his awareness, this book provides the opportunity to learn and subsequently create change. He is a committed lifelong learner, and he sets an example for all of us in our own commitment for personal growth.

The challenge? Each of us is on a different journey and at a different place. The messages have different meaning for everyone. Instead of telling you what to do—which is both easy and ineffective—this book leaves it up to you to choose both what you will take away and what you will do with it.

It is your choice. Will you be your best self for yourself and for the world?

—Cathy Liska, MCC and CEO of the Center for Coaching Certification

The *budo* arts (Japanese martial arts) cannot be practiced as a form of entertainment or distraction. They are a serious undertaking, which does not necessarily mean a sad one—far from it. You cannot approach them tentatively with your fingertips, with a mere touch of your lips, or with superficial layers of thought of heart. It would be better never to become involved, but if you do, it is essential to carry it to the end, until one's being is regenerated to the point of being human again, a real human.

As soon as your naked feet have entered a *dojo* (martial arts studio), you have entered forever. If you give up, if you waver, you risk finding yourself weaker than before—an important risk and a handicap that is difficult to compensate for. He who seeks, finds. The genuine masters do exist. Such a message of beauty and truth from the East brings an understanding to all those who are drawn and fascinated by the virile and knightly Way of Budo.

The Western mind has great difficulty in imagining how the idea of the sword, which represents purely a weapon of death, can be connected to a concept of wisdom and to a greater extent, the notion of *Do* (the way).

Yet the way of the sword surpasses traditional wisdom to which we are accustomed. It is greater than the idea of meditation, of deep personal reflection, of the recitation of the word, of self-denial, and of the ascetic image it assumes. In its true definition, it embodies all the most essential steps that Genaro shares in this book, taking their meaning to its ultimate conclusion.

We should not forget that the true meaning of Do lies in application combined with total self-commitment. His book also reminds us of the *ikigai* of budo, the main reason to live and the priorities to achieve. In Japanese culture, ikigai breaks down into different areas:

- What you love (passion and mission)
- What you are good at (passion and profession)
- What you can be paid for (profession and vocation)
- What the world needs (vocation and mission)

Once we have consciousness of our *satori* (enlightenment), we have our clear vision of where we came from, where we are, and where we will take our Do.

—Kenshi Shihan Sergio Cruz Belmont

Preface

To know and to act are one and the same.

—Samurai maxim

This book is about discovering your gifts, purpose, passions, and path to achieve your desires at your own pace. You will learn useful concepts to embrace a higher personal responsibility while truly enjoying your path, your truth, called *Do* (pronounced "doh") in Japanese. Once your Do is clear, you can empower others to clarify their Do.

I have worked with many CEOs and organizations for years and found that the common challenge resides in *how to create a powerful culture*: a culture with living values, with engaged people who pull the success of others, a magnetic culture that attracts more valuable people and boosts a virtuous cycle within the organization.

Many books talk about organizational culture—how to build an organization that lasts, overcomes challenges, and performs at its best. The question here is, whose best? The best of the organization, its collaborators, society, or shareholders? The approach of *this* book is to engage *members* of the organization to perform at a higher level. When both engagement and performance are high in all individual members of an organization, the organization as a whole moves toward its goals. It starts with our self-awareness, willingness to get better, commitment to pursue solutions, and acknowledgment that any change starts with each of us. It starts with me. It starts with you.

This book has a special gift, a tool that has proven effective for hundreds of our clients in their continuous growth: the Personal Strategy Canvas™ (PSC). The PSC is a tool for clarifying your deepest dreams, challenges, opportunities, and daily steps toward your goals. It includes everything, on a simple piece of paper. The main goal is not creating your canvas but the introspective discoveries you make while creating it. Let's find your inner motivation to ensure your success by creating and implementing your PSC. As you can tell, this book is about action rather than just planning and researching. This book is about doing, failing, learning, and doing it again to make a difference. I know this book will open vast possibilities for you.

Fifteen years ago, using my bachelor's degree in industrial engineering and master's degree in systems thinking and planning, I founded GTC Consulting, an international change-management firm that empowers individuals and organizations in the US and Latin America to achieve their goals. We have coached thousands of people to have a positive impact on their families and society. We focus on strategic planning and organizational development projects, collaborating directly with the executive level of organizations. Because of my engineering background, we emphasize follow-up and measurable results. This approach helps our clients achieve better results more independently. We also provide workshops in leadership skills development using experiential learning and executive coaching. This last piece has boosted our clients' results by developing them from within, raising the level of their accountability and focus on priorities. My professional career as an executive coach has been an amazing journey.

Nevertheless, I know my key to success has been my background in *budo* ("boo-doh"), Japanese for "martial way," referring to martial disciplines whose ultimate goals are spirituality, ethics, and self-improvement. Budo has developed in me great skills for life: discipline, passion, camaraderie, respect, honor, humility, and of course, leadership. Those learnings have allowed me to serve as *sensei* (teacher) for *karatekas* (karate practitioners) of all ages throughout the years.

Throughout my life, I trained with teachers in the traditional and philosophical side of Japanese martial arts, looking for opportunities to grow internally. Budo becomes a lifestyle and transcends the physical training. Traditional martial arts brim with millennia of wisdom on improving the character of participants to allow them to have a positive impact in the world. Through this book, I am living the dream of sharing the key lessons and insights from my experience training in the following disciplines:

- *Karatedo* (the way of the empty hand): For over thirty-five years, I studied this weaponless self-defense discipline that turns the body itself into a weapon. Beyond the punches, kicks, blocks, and self-defense applications, it also implies a complete philosophy for living life.
- *Iaido* (the way of the sword): During the last decade, I trained on the respect for and use of the samurai sword or *katana*. This discipline is also known as "the art of cutting ego."
- *Aikido* (the way of peace and harmony): Intermittently throughout my life, I learned to use locks, holds, and throws using the opponent's own force and movements. This discipline is often called "the way of peace."

Throughout this book, I will guide you in developing your own Personal Strategy Canvas™ (PSC) by sharing ideas, concepts, and stories from both my martial arts and business-development experiences. While some see me as an authority in some aspects of Japanese culture, martial arts, business, or leadership skills, I consider myself to be still learning. I just want to share with you this unique, hybrid perspective on self-development.

I truly believe we thrive by creating a memorable life. Understand your motivations for being here right now. You are reading this book for a reason; take advantage of this opportunity. This book is about sharing a passion I have had all my life, sharing how it has impacted my life, and ideally, inspiring you to improve your life and achieve your goals, too. I hope it gives you a profound approach to your self-development, leadership, and organizational growth. Enjoy it and use it as a guide. Commit to your own process, and you will see amazing things happening in your life.

Wishing you success!

Genaro Torres Celis
January 29, 2019

In true budo, there is no enemy or opponent. True budo is to become one with the universe, not train to become powerful or to throw down some opponent. Rather, we train in hopes of being of some use, however small our role may be, in the task of bringing peace to mankind around the world.

—Morihei Ueshiba, *The Art of Peace*

Acknowledgments

I want to thank all my friends and colleagues whose encouragement motivated me to work on this project. I also appreciate all the people who read the initial drafts and participated in many ways in this project. I thank all my instructors and mentors for giving me the foundation to undertake a project of this nature. My special appreciation to my teachers Antonio Belmont Cota, Javier Suárez Rocha, Sergio Cruz Belmont, and Cathy Liska because your lessons have been life changing.

I would like to thank Annella Metoyer and Jeff Toister because their guidance, resources, and perspective made this book possible. I want to thank Tom Bird for teaching me how to connect with my divine author-within state. Additionally, I would like to thank Denise Cassino and Fernanda Ramos for all the time, energy, and love supporting this project week after week. Special thanks to Tori Yabo for editing and reviewing all my manuscripts, for challenging me, and for all her teachings, professionalism, and passion about my message. My appreciation also goes to Laura

Gonzalez for sharing my ideas through her art with the cover of the book and to Chris O'Byrne for the book design and last details to have everything ready for publishing.

Thanks to my mom Patricia Celis de la Cruz, my dad Genaro Torres Alvarez, and my little brother Carlos A. Torres Celis, and my deepest gratitude to my life partner Paola Mora Reyes for all her love and patience as she waited during the weekends I worked on this manuscript.

Many people have shared their heart and spirit with me. Thank you for listening, sharing your thoughts, and keeping my motivation up. Thanks to all who join their path with me—you make this journey an exciting adventure. You know who you are, and you know you will receive a signed book from me expressing all my appreciation.

I want to acknowledge the following organizations that have built my character: Universidad Nacional Autónoma de México, University of San Diego, Casa Del Sol Karate-Do, Budo Iaido Zen, International Seishinkai Karate Union, Dai Nippon Butoku Kai, Center for Coaching Certification, International Coach Federation, Association for Talent and Development, and of course, GTC Consulting and Pupilo, where I focus most of my passion and spirit.

Introduction:
Where the Path Begins

Your work is to discover your work and then with all your heart to give yourself to it.

—Gautama Buddha

I was four years old when I saw something amazing, something that blew my mind. It was a group of people wearing white uniforms with black belts around their waists. Some had belts of other colors, but I only was paying attention to the ones with black belts. They were showing self-confidence and something else I couldn't describe. It was a sense of peace with power, a sense of focus with explosiveness. Nothing was important but what they were doing. They kneeled, stood up, and bowed to a person with a black beard in front of them, and then to all of us. We were just a bunch of elementary school kids. Our teachers had taken us to the main schoolyard minutes before our morning break. My teacher had said, "Be quiet—you will see an exhibition of a discipline called karatedo, a Japanese martial art."

I was riveted because of the way they were moving and performing punches, blocks, and kicks. I found it impressively powerful. It was like watching a movie with superheroes. At certain points, there were peaceful spaces, like during a thunderstorm when the rain is lighter, and just when you feel the storm is gone, a stronger thunderclap booms through the sky, the rain turns heavier, and your heart races faster until you realize everything is OK. I was having a blast—it was like being in the middle of an adventure, my heart pumping, my eyes wide, and my mouth, I can't remember, probably open.

I watched the karatekas fight each other, and at a certain point, a woman with a black belt soared with a flying kick across six people lying on the floor. When she landed at the other side, she broke three thick wooden boards using the edge of her bare foot with a shout: "*Kiai!*" The karatekas were very well-organized, moving together with a strength I didn't know was possible outside the movies. I knew a little bit about it because my dad had a book about karatedo, and I loved to look at the pictures over and over again. Now I was there, meeting the people in the book, with different faces but the same uniforms and belts.

I was just a little kid and easy to impress. For me, it was better than any movie or cartoon I'd watched in my short life, and this time, I was full of emotions—I was feeling something. I could smell the wooden boards, feel the noises. Their uniforms cracked in unison while they performed the same motions, and at certain points, someone was saying things I couldn't understand. It was the same karateka with the beard who seemed to be the leader, who later I learned was the *sensei*. He was giving the orders in Japanese and then counting: *ichi, ni, san, shi, go, roku, shichi, hachi, kyuu, juu* with the cracking of all the uniforms during each exercise, concluding each sequence with a "*Kiai!*" It was powerful—so much concentration, so much power, so much passion!

I noticed some kids were joking around, of course, and the teachers were saying, "Please be quiet." I was quiet. Nothing was distracting me at that moment. I was astonished, absorbing what I was seeing, trying to remember every single detail, the sounds of their uniforms and their exclamations of "*Kiai!*" coming not from their throats but from their guts. When that happened, their technique looked faster and more powerful.

They finished lining up, knelt, and closed their eyes. The sensei said, "*Mokuso!*" Everyone immediately closed their eyes and started to meditate. After a while, he said, "*Mokuso yame!*" They opened their eyes, stood up, bowed to the sensei, and then bowed to us in a way that felt like a thank you, or at least that was what I interpreted at that moment. It was so brief, so impactful in my mind, my body, and my soul. At the end, they smiled. They were having fun, and I had the sense that they loved what they did and who they were and just loved being there. I wondered who they were and why they were at our school showing their skills with a bunch of kids watching them in silence.

At that moment, I knew I wanted more of that feeling. I wanted to feel what they were feeling; I wanted to sense the floor with my bare feet. It was not enough for me to just look—I wanted more, and I wanted it now! I wanted to be a karateka. It didn't happen fast. I learned they were offering extracurricular classes after school, enrolling kids who wanted to join. That meant my parents would have to pick me up later from school those days, and we'd all have to eat later than usual. I didn't care, but my parents did. I started asking them day after day. I don't know how many times I said, "I want to train karate, please, please!"

Months later, I had my own little uniform and a long white belt that went around my waist twice. I thought it was too long, until I later learned it does go twice around the waist. I felt so proud; it was my first step. At that moment, I didn't know how this decision was going to transform my life. I just knew that every Monday and Thursday when the school alarm rang at 2 p.m., I had to run to the restroom, change from my school uniform to my *karategi*, do my best to tie my white belt, and run to the room at a corner of the elementary school. I had no idea I would be teaching there nine years later.

When I arrived alongside other kids, I couldn't imagine karate would become a passion, way of life, purpose, and beautiful discipline transforming the way I saw life, developing my character, and bringing the best out of me. I was just a four-year-old, about to turn five, who thought karate was fun and cool because of the kicking, punching, blocking, and moving fast. I didn't know there was something much more meaningful that was going to bring me joy and peace throughout my life.

During a class, Sensei Antonio Belmont said *karatedo* (the way of the empty hand) is about giving your best, growing as a person, and therefore, living your life with two simple principles: love and justice. Later, I learned it goes beyond that; however, for a little kid, that was enough information, something I could remember that I understood. I learned the techniques were just a way to achieve something deeper, something that takes a lifetime to understand and ingrain in your soul. During the years to come, I trained karatedo at different *dojos*, or martial arts studios, with Sensei Belmont. Now that I think about it, most of my trainings have been in daily life, applying the same principles and spirit taught by my sensei, teachers, mentors, and coaches. I made those learnings part of me, and the application has become like breathing. It is about flowing with life and being one with it to the point that there is no opponent, problem, or enemy against you, because you are one with them; they are just you. The aim is not to conquer the enemy but to conquer oneself. You reinvent yourself and give your best to grow and serve the people around you with love and justice.

You may train for a long, long time, but if you merely move your hands and feet and jump up and down like a puppet, learning karate is not very different from learning to dance. You will never have reached the heart of the matter; you will have failed to grasp the quintessence of karatedo.

—Gichin Funakoshi, *Karate-Do: My Way of Life*

Do: A Way of Life

Do not seek to follow in the footsteps of the wise.
Seek what they sought.

—Matsuo Basho, *Narrow Road to the Interior*

I n life, many circumstances drive change—change for
the good, for the bad, or just change. Many times,
the focus is much more on the goal than the path:
how we do it, why we do it, and how our actions serve a
bigger purpose. In Japan, there is an ingrained concept,
Do (pronounced "doh"), meaning the "way, path, truth,
or art." This concept gives much more importance to
the path than to other aspects of life. By focusing with
a sense of duty on little details step by step, day by day,
people can achieve greater things and move closer to
their peace of mind, their enlightenment, and their soul.

Do emphasizes total commitment to and
single-minded effort on the path of self-discovery
and self-actualization. That has changed among new
generations, with the influence of Western culture.

1

The concept of Do is alive in different disciplines like *karatedo* (the way of the empty hand), *aikido* (the way of peace and harmony), and *iaido* (the way of the sword). For example, *kara* (hand), *te* (emptiness), and *do* (way) combine to form karatedo (the way of the empty hand). Many understand it as how to defend without using weapons. But it also has to do with how to positively impact everything you touch. In this context, a karatedo practitioner is growing internally through the training of karate techniques, finding his inner peace. They are careful about etiquette, camaraderie, respect, discipline, honor, duty, compassion, integrity, humility, excellence, gentleness, and harmony. Living with Do is living a congruent life in which we are the living example of our values.

The Do is the way to become in alignment with ourselves; it is a call of duty to be a whole person. It is about taking in our hands our destiny, about acting with purpose. It is the way to enlightenment, not for the fact of being enlightened but to be one with the whole. Through the physical training, practitioners of Do achieve mental and spiritual growth. Concentration, focus, effort, a calm mind, and character-building are part of the training; however, it requires years to grasp the true meaning of the training, to really receive those benefits of being in the path.

In the word "*budo*" (Japanese martial arts), *bu* means "to stop a spear and quell the violence," or bring a natural balance both in conflict and out of conflict. In this context, the principles of Do are to attain a state of natural peace and harmony. Therefore, in budo, the real path starts when someone becomes a black belt, when one has proven to oneself the perseverance, focus, and will to achieve what is important in life. A true *budoka* or budo practitioner understands that even after training and getting better at their discipline after decades of continuous practice, the way to truly show mastery of skills is by the way of peace—the way of war is far easier than the way of peace.

Living Do starts with understanding why you are doing an activity, training, or practice and understanding your intention, your flaws, and strengths.

How strong is your will to do the following?

- Give your best effort to overcome your challenges . . . to overcome yourself.
- Grow and continue growing in all circumstances.
- Commit to continuously moving forward when situations are not favorable.
- Be humble to understand that once the path starts, it never ends.
- Let your Do guide all aspects of your life with principles, respecting yourself and people around you.

Your path turns into a way of life, as crucial as gravity or drinking water. It is about making sure you are making a better world. Living the concept of Do means growing yourself, second by second, to grow your society.

The Do concept has been with me in all aspects of my life, during training, studying, reading, interacting with others, and even walking. It is my way of bettering myself. I have also realized there are other ways to live the path, including other Japanese disciplines like *kado* (the way of the flower), *sado* (the way of tea), and *shodo* (the art of calligraphy). Any person can find the Do through devotion, respect, and congruency with family, colleagues, friends, or even strangers. Anyone can be humble enough to understand that the more we grow, the more we are aware of our flaws. Perfection does not exist; however, every single day, there is something to do for self-growth. It applies to many concepts, activities, and situations. One that I share in this book is how Do can be lived within organizations. "Organizational Do" is the truth and path of a company, nonprofit, school, or any team of people collaborating toward the same goal.

During all the time I have been collaborating with organizations, one thing is clear: The organization is a living entity and, like all living entities, must find its purpose. The complexity is higher because it is about all the people who bring it to life. Therefore, how much time should an organization focus on its Do? The organization's truth is relevant and very meaningful for everybody. What makes it unique? It is more than systems, processes, and operations. It is about the overall intention, its values, and how much those values nurture the mind, body, and spirit of its members. It is not about a specific person or a group of people leading the whole organization. Everybody is leading the whole organization.

So how can an organization cultivate its Do? Part of this multifactorial answer is by making the organization a place for skills development, a place for personal development for life, a place where all its members sharpen and discover their individual Do, collectively.

Skills, substance, and spirit without philosophy has no direction.

—Tesshin Hamada, *Quintessence of Japanese Classical Martial Arts*

Ganbatte: Give Your Best Effort

Victory is reserved for those who are willing to pay its price.

—Sun Tzu

In 2011, I was coaching Gonzalo Flechelle, an executive in Peru. It was a nine-month process, and during the first few meetings, the focus was on his business, how to empower his employees, and how to delegate and build a much more productive workforce to accomplish their corporate goals. The coaching relationship got stronger, so he started sharing personal goals and how he was going to enjoy life more and find balance as a whole person.

I asked him, "What do you want?"

He replied, "I want to enjoy life, be with my family, accomplish great things, and feel proud of myself."

"OK, what great things will you accomplish?"

He said right away, "I want to finish an Ironman!"

An Ironman is a grueling triathlon of swimming 2.4 miles (3.86 km), cycling 112 miles (180.25 km), and running a marathon—26.22 miles (42.20 km)—in that order and without a break. It is widely considered one of the most difficult one-day sporting events in the world.

I said, "Great! What is behind that idea?"

He said, "It's a dream, something I thought was for other people, something that if I do it, I will feel complete because it will fulfill my life. I want my family to be part of it. I want to feel that I'm capable of achieving anything I want. It's an idea that has been with me for a very long time but, well, I don't know . . ." He paused.

After a very long silence, I asked, "How will you make it a reality?"

He said, "What?"

I said, "Just answer the question—how will you make it happen?"

Then, another silence, a very long silence. I waited. It was a phone call, and I was starting to think we had lost the connection. Then he broke the silence:

"I was not expecting that question. Well, I will research a group I can join so I know what is required, and I will move on from there."

"That's a great first step. What will you do next?"

"Then I will start a training program."

"When do you want to accomplish those two steps?"

"Before our next session in a couple of weeks."

"How will you feel after accomplishing those first steps?"

"I'll feel great!"

"How will you keep your focus and motivation?"

The conversation continued until he created a detailed plan that was coming from deep inside of him without limitations or doubts.

In later sessions, he told me, "I know the Ironman is a crazy idea. It will require a lot of my time, and I will have to let go of other things. Do you think it's possible?"

I asked, "How much value will add to your life?"

"It will be awesome!"

"OK, it will add a lot of value to your life. You want to include your family. It will make you feel proud because you will prove to yourself that you are capable of achieving what you want, so what may limit your success?"

"Myself."

"How will you overcome that?"

"I will stick to the plan no matter what and use my coaching sessions to make sure I'm on track!"

The coaching conversation continued during the next sessions, and he shared progress in all his priorities at the corporate, professional, and personal levels. He made time to train for the Ironman. He saved some money, then bought tickets for the flights to the Ironman's location in Germany for him and his family. We finished the coaching process after months of meeting every other week, and life continued.

I was in a training session, and during a break, I turned on my Blackberry (yes, I know!), checked my email, and saw an email from Gonzalo Flechelle, with the subject "Thank you very much, I'm a finisher!" I started reading, and it was full of emotions, passion, joy, wisdom, hope, energy. *WOW!* I was reading it and felt dizzy. I had to stop and sit down on a couch to continue reading. My skin was gooseflesh.

This was his email:

From: Gonzalo Flechelle
Date: Friday, July 27, 2012 5:24 p.m.
To: Genaro Torres
Subject: Thank you very much, I'm a finisher!

Dear Genaro,

I want to share with you my experience in the Ironman last July 8.

You were one of the first people with whom I shared this idea, more than a year ago, when I was just processing the idea of what I had gotten myself into: the toughest sports test of all, an Ironman! I found in you a real support to believe in me as our sessions progressed, and we touched on the themes of personal goals and objectives. Remember?

The truth was that it was an amazing experience. One must live it to realize what it is about. CHECK IT OUT. Regardless of the distances traveled (which are already frightening), it is all that one is experiencing, living, and feeling from the preparation of months and months, the weeks before the race, the night before, the hours before, during the race (more than eleven hours!), the place, the smells, the people who support, what you eat and drink, what goes through your head, the landscapes, when you are about to arrive, when you arrive, the mixed feelings that I at least had never felt, etc.

To explain it better, I have cried a few times in my life, and they were all for sadness, pain, and powerlessness. When I was about to cross the finish line, a few meters away, out of nowhere and without being able to control it, I started to cry as if it were a sneeze, so suddenly that I had to rest my head on my wrists on top of one of the rails of a corridor through which those who arrived were passing. Suddenly I heard, "Hey, 'machine,' come, give me a hug." It was a two-meter-tall Spaniard—I did not even see his face—with open arms . . . I hung on to him like a koala for a few seconds . . . Then he passed me and went on his way . . . I had cried of emotion for the first time.

What does this leave me? A great teaching of life: that everything is possible, that we always must have something that motivates us to reach it, that fulfills us. That it is never too late to start anything and that one should *decide* it and *not stop* until it is achieved. In whatever—professionally, personally, athletically—in whatever! If not, life has no meaning. One is here to enjoy it, to live it—that is what it is about. Nobody paid me for doing this . . . on the contrary, I have spent a silver egg since I started over one year ago . . . but I can assure you that the feeling I felt is priceless . . .

Thanks again for the support, friend; I consider you part of my achievement.

Many successes.

PS: With lots of appreciation, I leave this photo of the "moment of glory," a few meters from crossing the finish line in 11hrs 52min 14 sec!!!
Gonzalo Flechelle P.
Porsche Manager, Euromotors S.A.

In his moment-of-glory picture, Gonzalo was running on a red carpet after having crossed the finish line, looking triumphant, proud, confident. Holding the Peruvian flag with one hand on each side, his arms were up in a V symbolizing victory, head tall, looking straight ahead with a smile the size of the world. On his waist, he was wearing a tag with his name and the number 1938. His sunglasses were on top of his white cap, and his entire body screamed satisfaction and happiness. He was truly enjoying his moment!

I was feeling joy, I was feeling alive, and I was very happy. My happiness was coming from knowing Gonzalo chose to make a dream true, and he did it! He was in a coaching process to boost his potential to succeed in his business and also at a very profound level, his personal life. He proved to himself anything is possible if he truly believes it. I loved seeing his picture with his arms in a V, with his face enjoying life—he did it. In his letter, he was thanking me and even wrote he considered me part of his achievement. I was like, *What!?* He did everything; I just asked questions, and he figured it out. He found his meaning. I was a strategic thinking partner to explore his priorities and most profound dreams. I felt so fortunate he saw it in that way, because he made me feel a part of it. I was proud of him, but most importantly, he was proud of himself, and he did it for him. How powerful is that!

Being a coach has paid off by far more than what I thought when I got my first certification as a professional coach. There is a lot of misunderstanding of what a coach is. In a nutshell, it is about letting the clients be the experts of their lives, of their own challenges. It is about letting them figure it out, find the power from within, find their own ways, and commit to their own solutions, their own paths!

Let me share with you a little secret, something that happened in my mind when Gonzalo said, "I want to finish an Ironman!" The first idea in my mind was *Wow, that's crazy!,* but my tone of voice and body language were still calm and focused. I was there to add value for him at every single second. As a coach, what I felt, thought, or previously experienced was not relevant. It was about him and how to serve him better. Of course, that first idea in my mind was coming from my own paradigms. I have trained in budo, and running, swimming, and going to the gym have been just a complement to my trainings and to polish my skills. So, swimming, bicycling, and then running for more than an hour is not my interest. But that is me from my own uniqueness, and the Ironman was his dream from his own uniqueness. There were times I wanted to share a thought from my perspective but then asked myself, *Will that serve Gonzalo?*, and the answer in my head was no. I was committed to serving him well and empowering him, letting him explore possibilities with his own thinking and his own ideas to boost his unique talents.

When someone actively listens to you, trusts in your skills and capabilities, how does it feel? Of course, it feels good, because we are awesome creatures capable of amazing things. It is just that, through life, we are continuously in contact with limiting thoughts: right versus wrong, easy versus difficult, one option versus the other. There are limitations, I totally agree, but who sets those limitations?

It is about you and your own goals. If it is about others' goals, they are responsible for setting their own limits. It is our duty to believe in our awesomeness and the awesomeness of others. Who are we to set limits for other people? We don't have any right to do so, even if it is a person close to us. We are limitless when we flow and let our mind, body, and spirit talk, sing, dance, paint, play, and shine toward our own purpose. Let other people shine, too—even more, empower them to shine!

A powerful Japanese concept, *ganbatte* ("gahn-bah-teh"), is an encouraging word to give our best, that anything is possible, and to never give up. It invites finding a solution to any challenge, situation, or problem. Every challenge comes with its solution. Sometimes we can't see it. Sometimes it's complicated to find it, but complexity doesn't mean impossibility. Every single situation has a way to overcome it. Gonzalo proved ganbatte. He knew what he wanted, he worked hard to achieve it, and he continued until he accomplished it. We all can attain whatever we decide if we are committed to never stopping or giving up.

Ganbatte literally is something between "you can" and "give your best effort." It opens your mind to possibilities and opens new paths. It implies life is in your hands, not in the hands of someone else, and you can have a direct impact on your results when you believe it. It encourages you to believe in a destiny you create. In any situation, there are variables that you can control and those you cannot control. It all depends on what you focus on. How good are you at differentiating them, at setting boundaries, at creating that image of the situation, and realizing where you can have a direct impact, an indirect impact, or no impact at all? It is about making peace with your situation, about both accepting and doing. You probably want it to be different, to be better. Everything is possible if you have the patience, the perseverance, and the clarity to accept your reality while continuing walking your path. Keep walking and stay focused. Do not expect anything—just do your best.

When you are certain, your actions will make a difference, and it's going to take time because it's a process. Ganbatte! Go for it. When you are passionate about your own dreams, there will be people feeling and living that passion. That dream will become their dream, too. Share your life in the same way you share time with family and friends, because being alive is not just to breathe, sleep, eat, and walk through life.

To be alive is living with intention, doing what you love, giving your best with the gifts you have, and sharing those gifts with others. Looking at yourself and smiling every single time, because you know you are awesome and you are capable of achieving anything you want. You just have to find the reason to act. Your inner motivation comes from clearly knowing your dreams and feeling them with all your senses, with your soul, while you speak. Everything is possible when you enjoy training and continuous practicing, when you walk your own path. Enjoy all the sensations you experience every day—the sweet ones, the bitter ones, the spicy ones. That mixture of feelings is called life. Enjoy it! Your happiness depends on the acceptance and approach to all those sensations. Be one with nature and appreciate it. Share your life with others, and make sure that you are living your life by continuously building your path with a clear purpose in your mind, your body, and spirit. What are you telling yourself? How are you training to overcome your obstacles?

You can give your best effort! Ganbatte!

To practice Zen or the martial arts, you must live intensely, wholeheartedly, without reserve—as if you might die in the next instant.

—Taisen Deshimaru, *Questions to a Zen Master*

Softness versus Hardness

Softness triumphs over hardness, feebleness over strength. What is more malleable is always superior over that which is immoveable. This is the principle of controlling things by going along with them, of mastery through adaptation.

—Lao Tzu

Softness and hardness are part of a balance, a constant transition between each other, a duality that complements itself. Even though I have been aware of this concept for many years, I realized that in many of my accomplishments I tried too hard, and by trying hard, I forgot to adjust or flow with a situation. Years ago, I visited friends in Portland, and we went snow skiing. I hadn't skied before, but because I like challenges, I thought it was going to be a great opportunity to learn and have fun. During the first couple of hours my friends were teaching me, my knees were hurting, and I was making fair progress. They wanted to take a rest, but I was having fun because I was falling less often, so we continued. I had had an experience before while learning to surf, when I'd practiced for many hours in a row until I made it, like a beginner, of course, but I was surfing. I was now applying the same intensity to learning snow skiing.

I didn't realize it was getting darker. We had been skiing for at least seven hours, and my knees were hurting, but during my karatedo trainings, I learned the mind is powerful enough to overcome physical pain. So I told them, "Let's go down one more time!" It was late. They told me it was dangerous. They looked tired, and I was, too. Even though it was night, it was illuminated. I told them, "Just the last one." They looked at each other and said OK.

I was the first one to go. Considering it was my first time skiing, I was skiing pretty well, but I noticed the snow was not soft like earlier that day. It was hard, more like skiing on ice than on snow. I got too much speed, and my knees were hurting even more. I lost control of my speed and direction. I decided to stop on my left side. I was braking but was not stopping. I could feel myself sliding on the ice. Then it happened: My left ski crashed into a small piece of ice the size of a tennis ball hard enough to make my left knee crack and to make me fly through the air. I felt it in slow motion, and while in the air, I thought I hit my head because of the strong crack. Then I landed and rolled in the snow until I stopped and realized my head was fine. The pain was coming from my left knee. I could barely move it. I tried to stand up but fell again. I looked at my friends, and they were looking for help.

Finally, someone with a snow motorcycle picked me up.

I had tried too hard throughout the whole day and didn't let my body rest and adjust to the new training. I was skiing on hard ice instead of sliding on soft snow. All that "hardness" broke my left ACL (anterior cruciate ligament). The hardness of my mind broke it. I broke it. I wanted to achieve in hours what many people achieve in days, even months. It was too much for my knee, and because of my inexperience, I didn't have the skills to manage a harder surface. That accident was a big lesson for me. I knew I didn't listen to my body or my friends. They told me it was dangerous, and I didn't care.

It took me weeks to let the swelling in my knee go down and took me months to recover. During that timeframe I couldn't kick or practice karatedo as I did before. I realized that until my body healed, I was relegated to practicing a "softer" discipline. I started to practice yoga and was amazed at how stiff I was, even though I considered myself flexible. I was impressed by how weak I felt in certain stances. I hadn't developed certain micro muscles to balance my body and make me stronger. I looked at how the advanced students did everything with seemingly no effort at all. When I had heard about yoga or seen a class, I thought it was something simple because the cardiovascular work was by far less challenging than what I was used to. I even thought it was a training for older people or people that do not want to push themselves to the limit. I was wrong.

A professional yoga class is very challenging. All students are advancing at their own level with very high concentration to overcome themselves and with a high self-awareness of their bodies. They are aware of their own limitations, of how to train all the muscles and joints to work in harmony and how to balance the whole body in different stances with no effort. It was challenging for me and at the same time, I was learning a new approach: to listen to my body and really take care of it. I learned that, over time, softness wins over hardness.

During that period, I was hurting my knee repeatedly in karate training because my ACL was not there anymore. It took me five years to have surgery to replace my ACL, but that is part of another story. I continued training karate, but I couldn't perform many of my advanced techniques. I felt I required that challenge, and every time I pushed myself, I hurt my knee. For that reason, to complement my karate trainings, I decided to practice a softer discipline, but yoga was not giving me the experience I was looking for. As a *budoka* (budo practitioner), I wanted to continue polishing my martial skills. For years, I had wanted to train *iaido* ("ee-eye-doh"), and now I was ready to start. Iaido is a discipline of learning to use the *katana* or samurai sword. It is a discipline where concentration, tranquility, and precision are vital.

Iaido is a training that focuses on the way of mental presence and immediate reaction.

The goal in iaido is to cut ego and make profound transformations in the practitioners' lives. Every cut has a purpose, conscious or unconscious, but what is clear is that we are making transcendental cuts in our lives. We are letting go of what is not necessary. During that process, we are becoming one with the sword and the sword with us. The level of awareness is different than in karatedo. For example, in karatedo, a mistake usually means receiving a punch, a kick, or a fall on the floor. The worst consequence is a knock out or hurting our bodies. In iaido, the self-awareness is higher—a swordfight is a life-or-death situation. There is no armor, and the focus of the training is self-control. It is a process that cultivates mental patience to keep the blade inside the *saya,* or scabbard. The mindset during our training is connected with both our Do and with our final departure. It is about finding our truth. The practice of iaido has a profound spiritual dimension. Even though iaido is also a martial art, the focus is more on softness because a strong motion doesn't cut. When the motion is soft and smooth like Japanese calligraphy, then the cut is effective. It's about merging with our surroundings and being completely present in our practice, our present.

I started training with Nakamura Sensei in both aikido and iaido. The beauty of it was that I continued learning and polishing my aikido skills, with both disciplines complementing each other, both focusing on softness over hardness. The principle underlying aikido is to use the full momentum of your enemy and merge with them in a very soft and fluid way to use their own strength against them. It is to yield to an oncoming force in such a way that the enemy is unable to harm you. The *aikidoka*, or aikido practitioner, changes his direction to push the opponent from behind instead of attempting to resist him from the front like karatedo does. The aikidoka never goes against his opponent's strength. Rather, he directs the strength away from him. I found it very interesting how I was breaking paradigms of what I'd learned in karatedo, which is much more powerful, but in the end, is simplistically strength versus strength. Now I was learning how to beat strength with softness. During my trainings with Sensei Nakamura, there were times I felt I had to unlearn what I knew to continue advancing with my aikido and iaido practice. Later I understood that it is not about unlearning but about accepting additional ways to do things. Like in mathematics, there are other ways to solve the same problem, to achieve the same goal.

Similarly, in iaido, Sensei Nakamura's focus when making an effective cut was in flowing with the enemy to use his momentum or speed against him—I learned from so many similarities with aikido. Both arts focus on softness, on being in a place where you flow with life and become the air, to the point that the katana cutting the air makes a sound that empties the mind and elevates our consciousness. I always have appreciated iaido and the beauty of a katana. I wanted to make it an extension of my body, to flow with life, and to cut what was not necessary or valuable in my life. The beauty and refinement of the steel blade are like a sunrise from a mountain when it leaves the *saya* (scabbard) and like a sunset when it gently returns.

Iaido is a lifelong practice, but it can be explained with five basic concepts: *kokyu ho* (breathing), *nukitsuke* (drawing), *kiritsuke* (cutting), *chiburi* (shaking off blood and cleansing), and *nohtoh* (returning the sword to the scabbard). Even though those concepts sound simple, many more details are needed to execute an effective technique. Iaido is about being completely aware of your body, surroundings, feelings, and emotions, and at the same time being at peace with what you are doing and who you are. The level of detail, precision, and control in every single motion is what makes iaido a beautiful art. The breathing must be done from the lower center of the stomach, and the sword must "breathe" together with the sword bearer. The stances focus on flexibility and control. All techniques must flow naturally like the waves of the ocean, and after the final cut, we cleanse the blade. We cleanse all thoughts in our mind—the ultimate purpose is the cleansing of the spirit.

Later I moved to another city and had a conversation with a friend who had studied karatedo with me years ago when we were in college. I told him that I was looking for an iaido sensei to continue with my practice, so he introduced me to Shihan Cruz ("master instructor" Cruz). My friend referred to him as *Kenshi*, Japanese for "master swordsman," but in iaido, it also means "sword saint" and is a name given to the founder of a school.

My friend asked Kenshi if I could attend a class, and I was invited. I attended an introductory class, and from the moment I arrived, I liked the feeling of the *dojo*. It was in a room inside a park, with mats on the floor. All students were wearing blue *hakamas*, big Japanese pants, and blue *gis*, martial arts jackets. They were not training with a *shinken* (real sword with the capability of cutting) or *iaito* (sword without sharpness), but with a *bokken* (a wooden sword). While training with a bokken, the risk of an accident is decreased. It is a great way to learn footwork, control, coordination, and focus. Yet the wooden practice sword can be as lethal as a real shinken because the true power is coming from the right execution of techniques. The main point is to make the practitioner become the sword. To train with a bokken must be like training with a shinken, and to train without a weapon must be as though training with a shinken. After years of practice, when a practitioner is ready to handle a shinken, his or her mental consciousness is already elevated to cut through personal fears and weaknesses.

During that first class with Kenshi, I noticed some differences from my previous trainings. Sensei Nakamura focused more on the martial side of it. It was about survival, life or death, speed, and precision. With Kenshi, the same concepts were there; however, he had a gentler way of teaching. His focus was more about polishing the spirit, about developing other samurai virtues such as premonition, precognition, intuition, knowledge, and wisdom. It was more than being effective with the sword. The etiquette of the class was more traditional, with much more focus on the details. It was not about the skills; it was about the being. In that first class, we practiced some *katas*, detailed, memorized patterns of movements. Some of those katas I knew to some degree, and other ones were completely new. Everybody was saying the names of each stance and movement in Japanese. The katas were new to me, and the names were not familiar.

I was following the class, giving my best, and at the end, Kenshi asked us to line up at the back of the dojo. Then he called on me and said, "Please perform all that we did in the class today."

I felt nervous, a feeling I hadn't had in a long time. I knew I could do it, and I did, at least to the best of my understanding. Even though I had trained karatedo, aikido, and iaido before, most of what I did in the class that day was new for me. So I was a beginner again, discovering a whole new world. When I finished, I was proud of myself. I knew I had made some mistakes, but I had given my best for that moment.

He looked at me, smiled, and with a very gentle motion of his hand, said, "Again, eyes closed."

At that moment, my mind freaked out. My body was calm because I have been training it for many years, but deep inside of me I was feeling nervous and completely out of my comfort zone. I knew all the advanced students were looking at me. I was new in this class, but some of them had trained with Kenshi for over ten years. I made sure my posture was right, breathed in, exhaled, and closed my eyes. Then I started. I wanted to open my eyes, but I didn't. At one point, I lost my balance, and when I finished, I was not sure I successfully ended facing where I started. I opened my eyes, and certainly, I was facing another direction.

He smiled and asked us to line up to finish the class. I was still assimilating what happened. *Was it right? Was it wrong? What do I have to improve? What do I have to practice until next class?* I wanted to be part of his class but didn't know if he was going to accept me. We sat down and started to meditate. Then he said, "Mokuso yame," and we opened our eyes.

Kenshi looked at me and asked, "What did you learn today?"

I thought I had more questions than learnings. After thinking about it, I said, "Kenshi, thank you very much for letting me participate in your class. I really hope you let me train with all of you. What I learned today was that even though I had trained for some years at another school, I'm sure my path is just starting. I'm looking forward to learning from all of you."

Kenshi said, "We would be happy to have you." He was going to move on with the next student, but I raised my hand.

"Kenshi, I want to keep practicing what I learned today. Where can I look for those katas, so I can train at home?"

He said, "Here! We train katas from other schools, and we train our own katas. You will not find them out there. It's not about showing that off to the world. It is about making them part of your being, like eating, breathing, and sleeping. I even encourage you to resist looking for techniques on the Internet because it may bias your own process, your own learning. This is the language of the body. Your body, your mind, and your spirit will get it over time. Just come to train and practice what you remember. If you remember just one thing, practice that repeatedly until you master it. Be consistent and respect your practice—it's a natural process."

I nodded in thanks. "*Arigato gozaimasu.*"

It kept me thinking . . . I had been training karatedo for over thirty years and had never seen it in that way. Before, I was studying, writing, practicing, and putting in a lot of effort to remember techniques to get better. His approach was about self-discovery, self-wisdom, self-knowledge, self-awareness, and self-consciousness. It was about me, not the other students, my background, my past trainings, or something else. It was to be in the moment, committing with myself, and giving my best with what I had today. The moment I had closed my eyes while training was like entering a new dimension, a new way to see, feel, and even smell life. Everything was different, starting with my emotions.

It was about being one with my environment. I was starting a new beginning. A new path was opened to continue progressing toward my main goal: to be one with my surroundings, to make a difference in my life and the lives of people I know, to be in a place where the mind is one with the sword and the body, to become one with emptiness and be emptiness. I wanted to learn how to make a profound cut on my habits and how to use the new iaido training as a complement to my karatedo and aikido trainings.

Hardness and softness are concepts that complement each other; one cannot live without the other. The more we practice both, the more we will be ready to overcome our challenges. Life is not about extremes; it is a dance of balancing opposites. During the last few years, I have been working on balancing what I think and do. I have been striving to be ready for any situation with a hardness without rigidness and a softness without weakness. The art is in finding the right balance in our lives, one that grows out of the unconscious. Every single action has an intention, an intention to get better, to let go what is not necessary in your life, to embrace happiness, peace, and harmony.

Kindness in words creates confidence.
Kindness in thinking creates profoundness.
Kindness in giving creates love.

—Lao Tzu

Kara: The Emptiness to Learn

The purpose of training is to defeat yesterday's understanding.

—Miyamoto Musashi, samurai and philosopher

When I was a kid, I asked my karatedo sensei, "What are the meanings of the belts?"

He said, "A long time ago, there were just two belts: white for beginners and black for experts. But it took three to seven years to develop the skills to become a black belt. Through the years, to keep beginners motivated, color belts were implemented."

Then I asked, "What is the meaning of the colors?"

He explained with an analogy I haven't heard or read any other place:

"Imagine you are inside of a cave. You can't see anything, and you continue walking, falling, and trying to find light. You are trying to see. Then you see a light far away, hesitate, and then continue walking faster. Eventually you can see your steps and your hands, so you continue walking, and when you get out, you see just white. It is too much light for your eyes. It is a completely new experience. You start to explore and learn about that new environment. That is when you become a white belt—when you start acquiring new knowledge in a different environment you are not used to.

"Then your pupils start to adjust, and you want to see where that light is coming from, so you look at the sun. It hurts, because growth hurts. You're out of your comfort zone, discovering new things, learning, and adjusting. You are certain the sun is providing light and warmth. You start to understand your surroundings, gain a new level of understanding. At that moment, you are a yellow belt.

"You still don't know where you are. Then you look at your feet and see you are stepping in something green. You kneel and touch the green grass below your feet. Now you are a green belt and have so much space to enjoy in this new environment of self-discovery. At this moment you are expanding your knowledge, you have more freedom, and you have new challenges and more risks. This freedom is coming with more responsibility.

"Then you scratch the floor and see the brown ground. You scoop it in your hands, and it collapses into many pieces. You look around and see the roots of the brown trees. Now you are a brown belt. You have a broader understanding of where you are and how to survive. You still have much to explore. You see the sky, you climb the trees, and you adjust to that new environment that you continue mastering day after day. It is a continuous discovery, a self-growth that never ends."

He finished, grabbed my shoulder, and looked at my eyes.

I asked, "And the black belt?"

He smiled, then continued:

"That's the moment you go back to the cave and start your real path through life. A different training, a most profound path of self-discovery. You already understood what you can see, feel, taste, smell, and touch. Now is the time to explore and learn what you cannot experience with your five senses. It is the moment you decide to live out of your comfort zone and make it part of your life forever.

"Many practitioners believe a black belt is the end of the path—that is a big mistake. A black belt is when your real learning starts, when you can understand what is behind the techniques and physical skills. When it becomes a lifestyle. When you understand all those years of practice were key to understanding emptiness. The more you learn, the more you must open your mind to new knowledge because the more you learn, the more you are a beginner at the next level of skill. It is a continuous path. Sometimes you go back to the light, and a new cycle begins. With time, your black belt starts turning white because of the erosion of use over years of continued practice. It is a reminder that humility is the foundation of everything. You will always be a white belt, you will always be learning, and you always can polish your skills, your mind, and your spirit. It is a reminder that any person can teach you a lesson. After many years of experience and practice, when you get older, you will be wearing a white belt. The same black belt will now become white because you will finally close the cycle. You finally become a white belt."

When I listened to it, made a lot of sense. I wanted to be a black belt, to discover the cave. I knew it would be so cool to be a black belt! That's what I did, and it really took me many years to truly understand what he was teaching me that day. What I did understand was that being a black belt was not the end of the path but the beginning of it. Today, with a smile on my face, I can say he was completely right. The path has been amazing. My self-discovery has expanded at many levels. I've been inside the cave, going out for resources occasionally and then coming back to continue my self-discovery, to continue discovering what is inside of me.

I can even say that my biggest challenges are not at a physical level. They don't have to do with techniques and self-defense. They have to do with feeling comfortable being uncomfortable, living with uncertainty, not knowing what is coming next, living in the moment. Further, they have to do with planning and being ready for the unexpected, adjusting and flowing when the unexpected is here. It is important to be calmed and in peace with a deeper understanding of what really matters in my life. I have realized that my karatedo trainings were just the surface of a deeper exploration.

Now that my body has more limitations, my mind is in better shape than ever, my spirit is full of joy, and the cells of my body are smiling.

Humility and learning go hand in hand. It sounds easy but requires a lot of self-awareness and the willingness to let go of past knowledge to let the new knowledge enter your life. If your cup is already full, the new knowledge will overflow from your cup, from your mind. The analogy of the cup comes from an old story shared by writer and martial artist Joe Hyams in his book *Zen in the Martial Arts* about a university professor who came to visit a Japanese Zen master. From the beginning of the conversation, it was clear the professor's real intention was to show his proficiency on the subject. After a while, the Zen master invited him to drink some tea. The professor continued talking. Then he saw the master pouring until the tea was overflowing the cup.

He told the Zen master, "The cup is full—no more will go in."

"Like this cup," the master said, "you are full of your own opinions and speculations. How can I teach you Zen unless you first empty your cup?"[1]

We must empty our minds every time we want to learn something new. The moment we believe we know it all is the moment we stop growing and start dying. The more we experience emptiness or *kara*, the more we will be able to grow and reinvent ourselves. The concept of Zen is about nothingness. As explained by the president of Honbu Dai Nippon Butoku Kai, Tesshin Hamada, in his book *Quintessence of Japanese Classical Martial Arts*, "It is so simple of a truth that we can recognize it without faculty of recognizing it. It is almost like asking the ocean, 'Do you have a mind?' And the ocean splashes your face with salt water and utters no words. Zen essentially refuses to be defined by any human terms."[2] Zen describes nothing and therefore proves nothing. The more we discover, the more we do not know; kara is present. Zen simply speaks without words, focuses on the core existence, and navigates the fundamental question of why. When we practice the Do aspect of a discipline, it is vital to empty our minds so we can see and feel with natural intuition. The spirit of Zen is transmitted intuitively, so it is necessary to go beyond our conditioned physical and mental barriers. Humility is vital to continuously learn, to seek for knowledge that goes beyond what we can perceive.

It is possible to master techniques without understanding or absorbing the spiritual and philosophical basis of what we do. It is also possible to apply the spiritual precepts of Zen without involving ourselves in the martial arts. Spirit is as important as technique. Soft skills (like people skills, character traits, and emotional intelligence) are as important as hard skills (understanding and proficiency in activities that involve methods, processes, procedures, or techniques).

The more you are open and aware of that balance, the more you will learn, and the more you will be ready to receive all the gifts the universe has for you. Empty your being and embrace kara.

> *The way of the sword and the Way of Zen are identical, for they have the same purpose; that of killing the ego.*
>
> —Yamada Jirokichi, official headmaster of *kenjutsu* (swordsmanship)

Your Personal Strategy Canvas™

*If you always put limits on everything you do,
physical or anything else, it will spread into your
work and into your life. There are no limits. There
are only plateaus, and you must not stay there; you
must go beyond them.*

—Bruce Lee

Living on Your Own Terms

Our society has very high standards, but who is really setting those standards? Those standards were set by others, and you can set your own. Of course, your environment plants ideas and paradigms in your mind. But you can either follow them or not. It is completely your choice. Because we live in a society, it is normal that we want to conform with others to be part of it. That's OK, if at the same time you are creating your own inner world, your own belief system, your own ideas, the freedom to create new paths, and the courage to walk all those paths.

In doing this, you are freeing your soul to become who you are really meant to be. We grow through exploration, by letting ourselves be free without being afraid to make mistakes.

What mainly limits our growth is our fear of failure. Conversely, we are afraid to succeed because that will be accompanied by more responsibility and will require more accountability in that new level of success. As you have been discovering, it's about a journey—a journey you create. There is a path you decide to walk or not walk every single day, but in the end is yours. You can run it, walk it, swim it, or ride it in any way you want. It's about you, not about what others are saying or what the people around you expect from you. It's about living in the moment, flowing, enjoying, struggling, overcoming, learning, and building through the process all the skills, habits, and wisdom to continue moving forward. Now imagine you create a new self-development system in which you do the following:

1. Define a clear vision of your future.
2. Discover your purpose.
3. Clarify the values that guide your decision-making.
4. Confront yourself to understand your strengths and flaws.
5. Take advantage of your opportunities and neutralize external threats.

6. Create goals for your self-development and professional development.

7. Build positive affirmations that will motivate and guide you through your path.

8. Establish your priorities and where to focus every day to achieve your goals.

9. Become a change-management expert, mastering the art of changing your life.

10. Open communication with the people who know you the best and start learning from them with humility, camaraderie, and respect.

11. Commit to slight changes every single day as part of your continuous practice and continue your path in all circumstances.

12. Achieve what you want because you are committed to your daily training. You are learning from your mistakes, and you are making progress every day.

Now is the time to move on from learning into doing. During the previous chapters, you have been reading, thinking, and learning some concepts that can be valuable if you start practicing them until you master them. You will continue reinforcing those concepts and learning budo wisdom. Now is the time to grab a piece of paper and start writing down all your ideas. Turn them into a plan. I strongly recommend having a notebook handy while you continue reading. It will help you keep your ideas together and will make more enjoyable your Do, your own truth.

> *When you are content to be simply yourself and don't*
> *compare or compete, everybody will respect you.*
>
> —Lao Tzu

Strengthen Your Roots

When we see a healthy, leafy tree full of life and growing strong, we might admire it or even want to hug it for a moment. It is comforting to touch the trunk, feel the textures, smell its many fragrances, and have lunch or read below its shade. We might visit a tree like that occasionally because there is something that attracts us, something beyond what our senses perceive. It's alive. There is magic around it, the magic of life, the "force," God, or Mother Nature, something beautiful that also makes us feel alive. What we can see is not the most beautiful part of the tree. What we are seeing is the consequence of something deeper, imbued with life, something trying to reach the center of the earth, the center of its own universe: roots.

Occasionally you can see those beautiful roots above ground. Sometimes you can touch them. But these roots grow stronger and deeper beyond what we can see. Those roots have been feeding the tree since it was a little sapling. What is making that tree gorgeous is not what we see but what we don't see. What we don't see is by far more powerful than what we are aware of. Other trees may be wondering, *Why is that tree that gorgeous? What is its secret?* The big tree is humble enough to just stand still under any circumstances, knowing that its greatness doesn't reside in the superficial but in the constant and continuous focus on what really matters, on its roots. There are situations out of its control, out of its reach, that it can't change or even influence. It can only focus on growing its roots to be more prepared for difficult situations, for times of scarcity. That tree has built a strong foundation to be part of an ecosystem. It is one with life, with the landscape, and it flows with the wind and the rain. It accepts and welcomes the birds and animals that live there or visit. It protects with its shade that person reading a book or that couple giving a kiss to each other with a glass of wine. The roots of a tree make it unique. It doesn't matter what kind of tree it is. It is unique, and it is beautiful.

That gorgeous tree is just showing a part of itself, a very beautiful part. If that tree were a person, we would see their body. It could be strong, athletic, healthy, and imperfect in ways that make it who it is. A person has a mind that is learning and is challenged to face infinite different situations. They also have emotions and feelings. Sometimes these benefit that person, and sometimes they work against them. Finally, they have a spirit that is tied to strong beliefs, values, congruency, and the legacy they will leave behind. All those aspects are their link with life and with the universe. How much attention is that person paying to all those aspects? What makes a person amazing is the level of commitment to strengthening their roots.

You also have roots. You have a background, studies, experiences, failures, and achievements. All these together impact your branches and leaves, your body and results. You may want to keep hidden what others cannot see. Whatever you do, your body and emotions will be the first window to reflect who you are. You are systemic, and all aspects of your life are important. The challenge is to balance all those aspects. To have adequate balance, it's important you truly understand your priorities. Your desires, dreams, thoughts, feelings, spirit, and beliefs are part of those priorities, your roots. The next chapters will dig deeper into your whole being: your dreams, purpose, self-knowledge, and environment knowledge.

FIRST DAILY CHALLENGE

Grab a piece of paper, answer the following question, and be as specific as you can:

- What are your roots?

Write down everything that comes to mind. Brainstorm. Whatever you write is great. Start and keep going on until you run out of ideas. Use all the time you require.

Even beneath a wonderful towering tree, in its roots lies a structure of struggle and perseverance.

—Morihei Ueshiba, *The Art of Peace*

Your Own Canvas for Success

Now is the time to start creating your unique Personal Strategy Canvas™ (PSC). I created the PSC for our clients years ago and have since used it in leadership development and coaching to transform lives. Take this opportunity and start transforming yours. It is not enough to think about your amazing plans. It is vital to write them down because it will connect with the part of you that learns kinesthetically. It will facilitate your follow-through. It will let you monitor progress and give you visibility of your path every time you update it. You are moving forward, and you are leaving a record of your path. If you track your progress, you can change, and if you change, you can improve. Your PSC will fit on a simple piece of paper yet will have everything you need to keep you on track and focused on what is most meaningful for you. Are you ready? I am sure you are.

Your **Personal Strategy Canvas**™ is divided into four main parts, and each part is divided into three segments:

I. **Visionary Mind**: Your behavior, purpose, and aspirations
    o **Values**: Your belief system that guides your decision-making
    o **Purpose**: Your path and main reason to live
    o **Vision**: Your image of the future

II. **Internal Knowledge**: Your uniqueness and inner motivations
- o **Strengths**: Your talents and what you have mastered
- o **Internal Goals**: Your individual and personal goals
- o **Weaknesses**: Your flaws and great masters

III. **External Knowledge**: Your opportunities and external motivators
- o **Opportunities**: Your possibilities to expand your results
- o **External Goals**: Your professional goals
- o **Threats**: Potential challenges to overcome

IV. **Execution and Focus**: Your priorities to achieve outstanding results
- o **Affirmations**: Your positive statements to keep you focused
- o **Priorities**: Your actions to reach extraordinary productivity
- o **Daily Focus**: Your daily actions for sustainable progress

As mentioned before, it is time to act. If you are deciding to continue and make a meaningful transformation through this exercise, grab your notebook or a piece of paper and create the layout that follows. You can also use the template at the end of the book or go to the official book website (www.dothepath.com or www.doelcamino.com) and download the fillable template. Schedule time to give yourself the gift of building your own path, of discovering your Do.

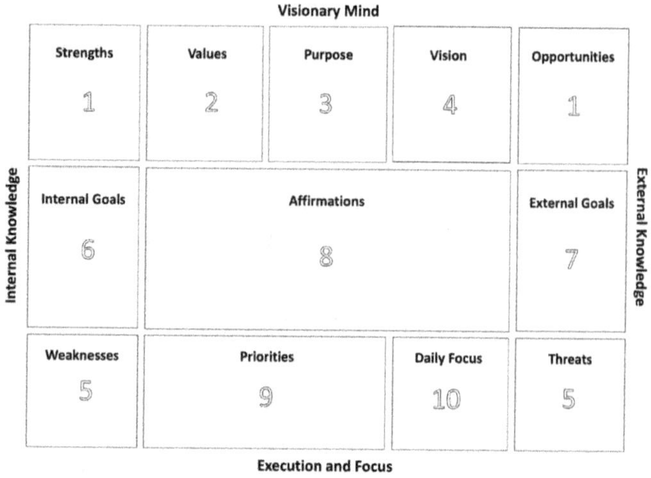

Figure 1: Personal Strategy Canvas™ (PSC)

You will notice the PSC has numbers—those numbers represent the order I suggest following. Through my experience I have proved that when people focus on the positive first, they are more creative, and their mind is more open to define who they are and imagine a phenomenal future. When they focus later on the parts of the PSC related to challenges, they already have enough perspective to create their goals and decide their execution plan. This is an iterative process, which means that once you complete each segment of your canvas, you might update your answers to the previous steps. For the same reason, it can be filled up in any order—it is completely up to you. The numbers are just a recommendation.

Another recommendation is to be honest when you write your feelings and inner motivations. Remember you are exploring your personal Do, your path, your truth. Avoid judging or criticizing your creation. It can be changed and adjusted at any time. It is a living canvas. You are giving life to it.

Any time you make considerable adjustments, create a separate new canvas with the new date. Keep track of your progress and review your previous planning until you get to the point that your PSC represents exactly what you want and where you want to focus. Remember that the achievement of your goals depends far more on this exercise than on your willpower. Once you feel clear on your PSC, it will be easier to be disciplined and keep your focus. Just be authentic and courageous enough to commit to your own success.

As explained, the following chapters follow the order I recommend. Just flow with it. Do not judge or criticize your ideas. Just write as fast you can and keep writing no matter what. The questions in each segment will be helpful for your brainstorming. Use a notebook or many pieces of paper to write down all your ideas before writing the vital information in your canvas. Before you start, let's explore ways to manage your energy and keep your vitality up throughout your path.

Manage Your Energy

To create and implement our PSC, we will need energy. It's one thing to clarify goals and plans; it's another thing to know how you will keep your motivation up throughout the process. As journalist Tony Schwartz and psychiatrist Dr. Catherine McCarthy explain in their *Harvard Business Review* article "Manage Your Energy, Not Your Time," one powerful way to focus your daily energy is to balance four aspects we will explore in depth: your mind, emotions, body, and spirit.[3] Each of these is directly related to how much energy you have while accomplishing your goals. It is crucial you focus as much on how to maintain high levels of energy as on how to live the life you want. Let's visit each of these four energetic aspects.

Mind

What makes us different from other species in the world is our capacity to think. Our minds can learn all kinds of information, and it is our responsibility to feed them in ways that improve our well-being. Every time we have a challenge and we figure out the way to overcome it, we feed our mind. Every time we learn something new or improve a skill, our mind is grateful. Unfortunately, many times we lose control of how we nurture it. There is a lot of negative or junk information that is not giving us any benefit. Think about the time you are spending on time-wasting activities and the time you spend learning or practicing something new. We all have time to invest or waste—we just need to gain control of it. To nurture your mind, please implement the following tips:

- Reduce interruptions while working on high-concentration activities.
- Establish time slots during the day to focus on low-productivity activities.
- Each day, identify the biggest challenge for the next day, and start your day with it.
- Estimate the time needed for each large task and distribute the work for each. For example, a priority may take you five hours, so you distribute it across the workweek, using one hour per day.
- Set daily meetings with yourself to work on your highest priorities and make progress. I recommend time slots of forty-five to ninety minutes without distractions.
- After working on high-concentration activities, give yourself a ten-to-fifteen-minute break and keep moving forward.
- Read, write, learn, imagine, create, listen, train, practice, and do whatever you can to feed your mind with quality information that will boost your growth. Limit or eradicate your exposure to all the junk information out there.

Emotions

As human beings, we have feelings and emotions. The capacity to deal with emotions varies from one person to another. Knowing ourselves means discovering what our triggers are to do some things but not others. Many times, our emotions lead our decision-making, and to find the balance, we must also use our logic. It is about disciplining your mind to discipline your emotions. Our emotions are influenced by several factors, and one of the things we can control is the way we create bonds with the most important people in our lives. Building relationships is key to enjoying life alone and with others. Here are some tips:

- Focus on positive emotions and use phenomenal words; use a language that inspires you.
- Learn and practice breathing correctly, especially when you are under stress; take long deep breaths.
- Express appreciation to others by all means possible (in person, notes, email, etc.)
- Engage regularly in meaningful conversations; connect at a deeper level with your loved ones.
- When in hard situations, practice different perspectives, put yourself in charge, and focus on the possibilities to solve it.
- Practice a hobby or an activity that inspires you; do what you are passionate about.

<u>Body</u>

As mentioned before, your body is the reflection of your attitudes and habits. We must train our bodies to do what will serve our goals. Our mind is always looking for the shortcut, and our body is constantly seeking short-term pleasure. But if we feed our bodies constant pleasure, we spoil it. Later, when we want to achieve something, our body will be used to that pleasure and will misbehave. An example of this is junk food habits or not exercising. It requires discipline to prepare a healthy meal and additional energy to work out. Sometimes it is effortless to keep our bad habits, but once we start new ones, it becomes easier to keep a good physical condition than to start over again. Many times, we have to do with our body what will benefit it, not what feels good in the moment. We must not do something only because it is fun but because we are teaching our bodies to do what is best for them, similar to when we educate our kids. The great news is that your body and your health will appreciate it in the long term, just as many kids appreciate childhood lessons when they become adults. Here are some tips to educate the body:

- Create a routine to go to bed and wake up, and make sure you sleep daily as much as your body requires.

- Reduce or eliminate alcohol, processed food, or any other junk food or beverages.
- Exercise and practice cardiovascular activities for thirty minutes daily or at least three times per week.
- Be mindful of the portions you eat, and have light snacks every three hours.
- Listen to your body and identify signs of hunger, sleepiness, pain, or lack of concentration. Visit a specialist if needed.
- Your body requires healthy food, exercise, and quality rest. All of them are important, so make sure to balance them.

Spirit

Many people associate spirit with religion. The idea of spirit can include religion and also go beyond it. Spirit is about leaving a legacy, living your life with passion because you have a clear purpose, acting congruent with your values, and naturally nurturing your soul. You nurture your spirit when you connect with nature and become one with your environment. Your spirit is alive when you link yourself with all kinds of energy, when your surroundings become your soul and your family, when you are certain the world is your spiritual home. Your congruency with your belief system and intended legacy is a key part of your spirit. You feed your spirit when you give the best of yourself to all people in all situations to transcend your life and the lives of others. Here are additional tips to guide your path:

- Practice activities that give you feelings of satisfaction, peace, and harmony.
- Save time and energy to relax, connect, reflect, meditate, or whatever works for you.
- Live your values, be consistent, and be congruent with your belief system.
- Have a journal and write about yourself, the important people around you, nature, and the universe. Feel free to pursue whatever you are expressing there.
- Connect with your environment; accept and respect the differences.
- Flow like water, accept what you can't change, and change what you can.

The balance of all those aspects will nurture your well-being. It will give you a deeper understanding of who you are and what will make a difference in your life. Be aware and conscious about all those aspects: what you can't control, what you can, and what you decide to do with what you can control. Those aspects will open new paths to evolve, to grow, to get to the center of what really matters to you. This is your life, and life is about being one with your surroundings. Strengthen your roots, and merge with your environment.

SECOND DAILY CHALLENGE

In your notebook, answer the following:

- Evaluate each of your energetic aspects, on a scale from one to ten: mind, emotions, body, and spirit.
- Create at least one action you will implement and sustain for each aspect. Start with the lowest rating of your self-evaluation and so on.
- For each aspect, answer the following question: How will I make sure I do it?

Enjoy your introspection and use all the additional time you require.

The next chapters will guide you on how to take the most advantage of your PSC in ten simple steps. Let's start your journey!

Step One: Strengths and Opportunities

A man who has attained mastery
of an art reveals it in his every action.

—Samurai maxim

Self-Mastery Is a Contact Sport

Self-mastery and the way of peace goes beyond budo. It's about knowing ourselves—our emotions, our feelings, and our frustrations—very well. It's about knowing what makes us happy or mad, knowing our strengths and weaknesses, and knowing how to use those strengths to better serve others. It's about taking responsibility for who we are and who we want to become. Self-mastery means understanding that nothing is still—everything is moving and evolving, even in the most difficult situation. We always have a choice to manage it differently, to seek a bright outcome.

In business, people talk about leadership skills; in budo, we talk more about self-mastery. This concept starts from within and is completely related to personal accountability. Some people understand personal accountability, but just a few really use it as a way of life. To be personally accountable, you must apply the concepts shared in this book:

- Respect others, be assertive, and adjust to the situation.
- Use your self-knowledge to add value with what you do and say.
- Focus on the solution and be part of it.
- Be honorable and responsible for your actions.
- Let your actions and results define who you are.
- Live far from your comfort zone.
- Be the driver of change, and ask questions to make others commit.
- Live your Do, your path, with discipline and passion.

The opposite of personal accountability is a person who constantly complains, points fingers, procrastinates, feels like the victim, is full of excuses, and is constantly looking for ways to avoid responsibility. That person can be me or you. We are all humans and have our flaws. What makes the difference is when we raise our self-awareness and catch ourselves in those sorts of attitudes and behaviors. It is common to behave that way because accountability is not something that comes naturally. It is vital to work continuously in our self-knowledge and constantly raise our self-awareness. It requires practice, focus, and an extra effort. When you practice enough, you make it part of you, like the air you breathe. Then you will notice it is easier to have self-discipline, to lead your life, and to add value to others. It is not a switch to turn on and off. Anytime you switch it off, you prove to yourself that you are not really walking your path for self-mastery.

You know you are making progress in your self-mastery when you know what you want and commit to it, when you make a difference in yourself and have an impact in others. It's like magnetism. You lead your life in such a way that inspires the unique paths of other people around you. When you progress in your self-mastery, you start being surrounded by people on a similar journey. People want to share their similar journey with you, and consequently you all share your paths together. When you work on yourself, magnetism increases. When you progress and put your ego aside, you attract valuable people around you. When you change, your world changes.

Many people spend all their lives trying to be someone else, trying to match other standards, or trying to change their surroundings instead of simply committing to change from within. We cannot achieve self-mastery, but we can have a daily progress in our self-mastery. We can work to ensure we are better than the day before, the month before, the year before, and the decade before. That is precisely the quintessence of the path: It is continuous, and it requires other people to make it alive.

Self-mastery is a contact sport because it is built through constant interaction with others, starting with setting very clear expectations and clarifying the main intention of every interaction. It is a contact sport not just because of the constant contact and communication with other people but because it requires training, and as with any sport, you must be psychologically ready. Just as in *kumite* (respectful sparring), you get better by giving and receiving. In this case, we are not giving and receiving punches and kicks but phrases and situations. Sometimes what you receive is unpredicted, like a sudden strike. Other times, a difficult conversation turns into kumite. Instead of using your self-defense techniques, you use your soft skills to deal with the situation. The other person may want to put you down, but it is not about what you receive; it is about how you deal with what you receive. How calm are you? How clear is your mind while dealing with the situation? During real kumite, whenever one of the opponents gets angry, mad, or upset, they have less likelihood to overcome the situation. Mainly it is because they lose focus. If you lose focus, the probabilities of being out of control are higher, and if that happens, you are raising the stakes against you. The only thing you can control is yourself.

Simply imagine you are a "mental athlete" in the Olympic games. The difference is that you are not necessarily competing against others—you are competing against yourself. Self-mastery and communication are merged concepts; both require constant training. In every interaction, you have the chance to do what you have trained. Train by making plans, attending workshops or classes, and implementing your PSC. You can also train kumite during meetings, one-on-one conversations, roleplays, coaching sessions, and your daily interactions. Once you open lines of communication with the people you interact with the most, put into practice all the concepts taught in this book, especially humility and learning. Kara (emptiness) will be a great ally during your learning process.

Assertive Communication

As a contact sport, self-mastery requires skills for dealing with various situations. One soft skill already mentioned is personal accountability, while another important one is assertive communication. Know who you are and what you want to get from any interaction. Have a clear intention in your communication. That will give you clarity about the mood, tone, words, body language, and many tiny details to be aware of when you are communicating. It starts with perfectly knowing the result you expect with the person or audience in front of you. Your intention must be clear because it will guide all your conversations.

Being assertive is understanding the difference between being passive (letting others overstep my rights) and aggressive (me overstepping others' rights). It is your capacity to balance both, based on the situation. It is also avoiding being passive-aggressive (where you let others overstep your rights and you overstep others' rights at the same time), which is the most dangerous circumstance because it erodes trust, blocks communication, and creates conflict. Being assertive is treating all your communication opportunities with the respect they deserve. We are in this world to connect and build meaningful relationships. Respect other points of view and be precise with your arguments. Every time you grab your phone, send an email, or talk to a friend, colleague, boss, or spouse, you are building your legacy and branding, and at an unconscious level, people are creating frameworks in their minds about who you are.

At the end, their perception about you is their reality and is as valid as your own perception of reality. Both perceptions are real and come from our own uniqueness. We interpret the world in different ways. Those perceptions may overlap with other peoples' but for sure are not identical. Now think about how many people you interact with daily and how many among those know you well. Have you seen a picture of yourself you don't like? You might immediately want to erase or hide it because it is not pleasant to see yourself through that angle. Well, something similar happens when you are recorded in video or audio for the first time—it's weird! That is the way people see you, listen to you, and sense your personality. For them, those angles are common, even if you don't like them. In some ways, they know you better than you know yourself. Continue thinking about this—we will dig further into this concept when we review weaknesses and threats.

THIRD DAILY CHALLENGE

Answer the following questions, write as fast as you can, and continue until you run out of ideas:

- When someone gives you feedback, what makes you feel uncomfortable?
- In which situations does your primitive brain want to react?
- How are your skills to handle those situations?

Your PSC: 1. Strengths and Opportunities

Strengths

When you start thinking about *strengths*, it's important to think about your talents, attitudes, skills, and habits that have been key for the achievement of your goals. A strength is an internal characteristic. It's probably something you have practiced long enough to turn it into a strong attribute, something that positively describes who you are. Consider what people appreciate about you. Have in mind that a strength can easily turn into a weakness when the "volume" is too high.

For example, self-confidence at a very high volume can turn into arrogance, or an organized person taken to an extreme could be perceived as obsessive. Write a list about your current strengths using the following questions and be honest with yourself. Later, you will create a list of the flaws you believe you have. For now, just focus on all your positive aspects, and use the following questions to help you with your brainstorming:

- What am I great at?
- What am I proud of myself for?
- What do other people admire about me?

For every strength you write, you should be able to provide several examples describing how it is appreciated by yourself and other people. Write the most important ones, a minimum of three and a maximum of seven.

Examples of strengths are: organized, proactive, disciplined, easygoing, resourceful.

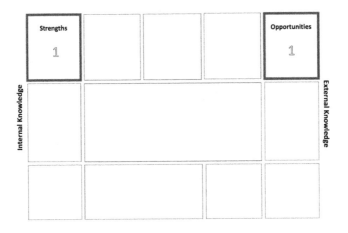

Figure 2: Strengths and Opportunities

Opportunities

In contrast, *opportunities* are related not to you but to your environment. Strengths are internal factors. Opportunities are external possibilities that have the potential to expand your results. If you decide to act on these situations, your reality will positively change. They align with how you imagine your future and nurture your definition of success. Write those opportunities as a first draft. You can revisit them later. Use the following questions to create a list of the ones that make you excited and contribute to what you want in your life.

- What situations can I take advantage of to grow?
- What is happening around me that I can benefit from?
- What could happen that may benefit me?

Write a minimum of three and a maximum of seven. Your first three must be the top opportunities you will focus on first.

Examples of opportunities are: get a scholarship for my master's degree, invest in a program for my self-development, volunteer with a philanthropic project, let my network know what I'm doing, and ask for referrals.

FOURTH DAILY CHALLENGE

Remember you are writing and consolidating all your insights before jumping into filling out all of your PSC. Progress is about doing rather than knowing. Stop to write down your strengths and opportunities, or schedule time to do all the exercises in this chapter. Whatever you decide, act!

Self-mastery is about discipline of thinking and discipline of action. It is about the decisions you make second by second. It means that you are leading your life and that there is a clear intention every time you do something, even the tiny little details. According to motivational speaker Mel Robbins's book *The 5 Second Rule*, it takes just five seconds to act and reclaim control.[4] Pushing yourself and showing your whole being who is in charge takes constant training of your mind, body, and spirit. Self-mastery is acting on what is relevant for your growth, choosing the quality of the information you are receiving, the food you are eating, and any other input—everything is relevant. The world has marvelous things to offer, but unfortunately it is also full of poison and junk. It is your responsibility to filter what you are getting and focus on the positive.

Now is the time to push yourself a little bit further!

The essence of warrior traits is demonstrated by: integrity with self, and honesty with others.

—Soke Behzad Ahmadi, *Legacy of a Sensei*

Step Two: Values

We should not seek victory over an enemy,
but victory over self through correct principles.

—Tesshin Hamada, *Quintessence of Japanese*
Classical Martial Arts

A Code of Honor

The samurai legacy is well known around the globe because of the courageous and highly disciplined ancient warriors who led the military in Japan from the seventh to the nineteenth centuries. The etymological definition of samurai means "being at one's side." Another interpretation of this meaning is to serve a cause. Samurais came from different social backgrounds (farmers, hunters, etc.), and they had outstanding skills in archery, horsemanship, swordsmanship, spear wielding, and more. A true samurai was a very educated person not just in the arts of war, but also in poetry, painting, history, and other fields. Samurai warriors were committed to their self-growth, so they could be socially acceptable in high court and better serve their lord. They were a class of warriors to serve the aristocratic nobility, and on some occasions, they had political positions. It is a common mistake to refer to all warriors as samurai. A true samurai had a spiritual morality, a code in his consciousness that addressed how he should live and how he should die. They had the same human characters of ordinary men, but they stood by their code of morality, which was greater than any written code.

It wasn't until 1900 that Japanese educator Inazo Nitobe wrote *Bushido: The Soul of Japan,* a book of rules of etiquette, respect, and loyalty for the samurai.[5] Some of the virtues a samurai adhered to were absolute honor, courage, self-sacrifice, rectitude, contempt of death, self-reliance, austerity, and relentless discipline. Death with honor was as significant as victory with honor. They had a very clear sense of their philosophy and values to live as an honorable samurai, a true *bushi,* or warrior. They lived by the following values:

- *Meio* – Honor
  Their focus was on self-improvement, and they did not seek judgment or validation from others. They owned their errors and did all that they could to make things right when mistakes were made.
- *Gi* – Justice
  Integrity and correct principles were essential virtues for the samurai. Their code emphasized

personal accountability, justice, commitment, and a sense of pride. They stood up for what they believed in and did what was the right thing to do.

- *Ju* – Heroic Courage
  They were confident and took risks because they knew that was the only way true growth was possible. They always strived for improvement and refused to settle. They did not back down or live in fear.
- *Jin* – Compassion
  They showed compassion and helped at every opportunity. They actively looked to improve the lives of others and make a difference in the world.
- *Rei* – Respect, Etiquette, and Courtesy
  They were gentle and displayed a balance between strength and humility. They valued quality over quantity and looked for what was best for all who were involved in any situation. They were kind and courteous even to their enemies.
- *Makoto* – Absolute Sincerity
  They were honest. If they said they would do something, you could be sure it would get done. They valued trust and would rather die than break that trust.
- *Chugio* – Loyalty
  They were immensely loyal to everyone who relied on them. They knew the power of

their words and actions and held themselves responsible for all the consequences of those actions.

Like the samurai, we must live by our own code of honor to guide us in our everyday lives. The people around us stay with us for a long time because we share similar value systems. The more your values are clear, the more they can guide your decision-making, and the more they will nurture your spirit. When your value system becomes the framework of your Do (your path), you will be much more successful in life because valuable people will be willing to collaborate with you. People with a poor value system or a lack of ethics will attract people with a similarly poor value system. A code of values details characteristics that are desirable in all aspects of your life. The samurai stood out from others because they lived and died by their value system. You can use the same guidelines to increase your overall well-being and performance. Polish your value system and be consistent under any circumstances. That will boost your success!

FIFTH DAILY CHALLENGE

Answer the following and be as specific as possible:

- Describe your own code of honor.

Perfect, let's dig into your value system.

Your PSC: 2. Values

Your values define the way you behave and the relationships you appreciate. They are the foundation of your belief system, which guides your decision-making. They mold your character and feel great in your heart and soul when you are congruent with them. They also leave you with a bad feeling when you behave in the opposite way because of your lack of coherence.

Values fall into one of two categories: unquestionable or desirable. *Unquestionable values* are binary; you either have them or not. In your belief system, a gradation or level of compliance is not acceptable for this particular value. For example, honesty, in your belief system, may be unquestionable because you cannot be a little bit honest or honest in some situations and dishonest in others. For example, imagine you are in a situation where you could steal to radically improve your life, and no one would know about it. What would you do? If you decide in such situations to still adhere to your value, you can say it is a binary value for you. However, if you feel it depends on how bad your situation is or how safe you would be going through with it, it is probably just a *desirable value* for you or not even a value to consider in your belief system.

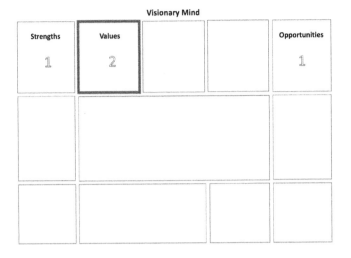

Figure 3: Values

Here you must write just your unquestionable values, those values that when someone close to you doesn't respect them, it is enough reason to question if you want to keep that person in your life. Your value system is one of the most profound parts of your PSC. If you want to write some desirable values that you want to turn into unquestionable values through the consistency of your actions, do so, but only after first writing your current unquestionable ones. Focus on your unquestionable values first by writing a minimum of three and a maximum of seven.

Examples of unquestionable values are: honesty, professionalism, respect, confidentiality, commitment, and continuous learning.

Be courageous, challenge yourself, and empower who you really are. Write them down, and even create your own definition for each one of them. Finally, live them and be the example of your own value system. You are always looking at yourself; honor yourself.

SIXTH DAILY CHALLENGE

After writing your values in your PSC, grab your notebook and do the following:

- Describe your own definition for each one of them.
- On a scale from one to ten, rate yourself on each value.
- Now think of the people closest to you (family, friends, coworkers, etc.) and rate them on average (as a group) on each value using the same scale.
- Analyze what you wrote. To live your value system more intensely, what will you do differently?

This is your code of honor. The more you raise your self-awareness and adjust, the more your soul will feel grateful for your actions.

An honorable warrior knows the true meaning of rectitude as it serves the source of his legitimacy and justifiable actions.

—Tesshin Hamada, *Quintessence of Japanese Classical Martial Arts*

Step Three: Purpose

Always be yourself, express yourself, have faith in yourself; do not go out and look for a successful personality and duplicate it.

—Bruce Lee

Your Personal "Do"

Your personal Do, path, or truth does not start when you start doing something new. Your Do starts when you prove to yourself you really found a purpose that fills your spirit. It begins when you have committed long enough with perseverance and discipline to really appreciate your own truth. When you find a path that nurtures yourself and is an integral part of your life, it can be a conjunction of many things. We really start walking our Do when we have a fair understanding of who we are and who we want to be. When we discover our inner motivations, accept who we are, and have a deep understanding of our priorities, we walk our path. We must commit our time and effort to focus on those priorities and make those priorities absolutely ours. More people can be included, but we set them with no external influence. We make our purpose part of our lifestyle, knowing that the path is so beautiful that the goal is not that relevant. Our daily path and how we live our purpose—our continuous growth—are what matter most. The goal of the past becomes the achievement of the present. Then a bigger goal arises, in a continuous cycle, but the goals themselves are less important than living our personal Do: our own purpose, path, and way of living life.

Life has taught us that results, achievements, and recognition are important. There is a tendency to replicate others' success. We have been taught directly or indirectly that our achievements will make us happy, but happiness is by far more complex than that. Our achievements make us feel good, but happiness is much more profound. It is about enjoying the path you built for yourself, the path you are continuously adjusting that is teaching you great lessons while you walk it. Happiness is building your personal Do. It won't be perfect. It will have challenges, surprises, ups and downs. But it is yours, and you are walking it. You can change it, fix it, and overcome any challenge you face. Once you create your path, you become the builder, engineer, and architect of your own life, building the life you love. The process requires consistent training—you will get better over time so naturally that you will be amazed at your progress.

When you focus on your personal path, new growth habits will flourish. You must be careful because if you work from your ego, frustration may arise. Do it because it is an enjoyable path you want to walk every single day, a purpose that inspires you to give your best toward your goals without worrying about succeeding or failing. When your main focus is on continuously walking it, over time, your Do compensates you with the natural rewards of all the passion, effort, time, focus, and patience you committed to achieve it.

Take the most advantage of your present and focus on moving forward. The past is your greatest teacher, and that's it. You are living the present, and life is too short to spend too much time in the past. It is too short to spend too much time in the future, and the present is just an instant that passes by so fast. Enjoy it or lose the moment. You can grow in any way you want, and one thing is certain: You are much more powerful than you think. You are unstoppable! Truly believe it. It is about knowing yourself, accepting yourself, embracing yourself, expanding your talents, and working in the areas you want to grow, step by step. It is simple—enjoy the present and make every moment count toward the future you are creating.

SEVENTH DAILY CHALLENGE

You are certainly walking a path:

- What do you like the most?
- What will make it more enjoyable?
- What changes will you make?

Good job!

Your PSC: 3. Purpose

At this point, you know what positively defines you and your belief system. Throughout this book, you have been exploring from many different angles the meaning of the Japanese word "Do".

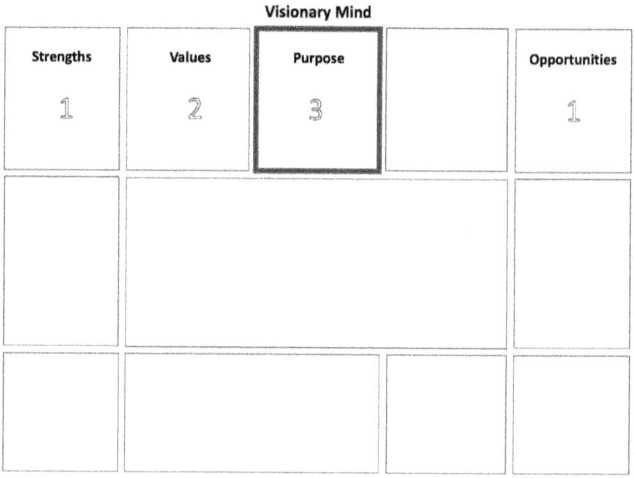
Visionary Mind
Strengths
1
Values
2
Purpose
3
Opportunities
1

Figure 4: Purpose

Your *purpose or mission statement* defines precisely your path, your main reason to live. It is what you do when you wake up and continue doing throughout your day. It is a way of life that keeps you moving forward toward your goals. Maybe now the path you walk every day is sometimes unclear, or you may be walking a path you are not enjoying. Maybe you are the opposite: You clearly know your purpose in life and what makes you enjoy every single day. Maybe you are already doing what is good for your body, mind, and spirit. Use this opportunity to evaluate and find the reason you are doing what you are doing.

Your purpose should be something easy to explain in a few words, and it must be simple enough to be understood by any person. To accomplish this, write it in approximately eight words, and make sure your purpose inspires you throughout your days. It must be a key component of your inner motivation and a resource to keep you inspired when situations turn complicated.

Examples of purposes are "to have a positive impact in society," "to be happy and spread happiness," "to be my best and serve others," "to live a positive and memorable life."

EIGHTH DAILY CHALLENGE

We all want to give results, but results based on what? Finding your purpose will nurture yourself. Answer the following questions and explore further about your purpose. I recommend working on it when you have no pressure about time, probably during a weekend.

- How are your achievements nurturing your soul?
- How much are you enjoying what you are doing?
- How connected are you with your environment and with yourself?
- How are you feeding your soul?
- Imagining you are the main character of your own movie, how is your character
  - Enjoying life?
  - Following their own passion?
  - Behaving?
  - Feeling?

How authentic is your character with their own truth? At the end it is not a character but you. You are performing your own life and creating your own destiny under your own circumstances. Imagine your life so far has been your own movie:

- What was the genre?
- What was the name?

Imagine today you start a new movie:

- What kind of movie will it be?
- What will be the new name?
- You are the main character. What will you do differently?

If you want to make it more vivid, create a mind map or paint yourself living your purpose.

Imagine your personal Do, build it now, make it vivid, and live it now!

Learn the form but seek the formless. Hear the soundless. Learn it all, then forget it all. Learn the way, then seek your own way.

—The Silent Monk, *The Forbidden Kingdom*

Step Four: Vision

Knowing others is wisdom, knowing yourself is Enlightenment.

—Lao Tzu

The Future You Create

Your image of your future is unique because you are your own universe with marvelous landscapes and scary places to visit. You are a great creation of this miracle that we call life. How often do you explore that universe? What parts of that universe do you know? What is unexplored? What parts do you share with others? All those hopes, dreams, habits, experiences, places, emotions . . . all of that is you!

Until this part of the creation of your PSC, you have been digging into your strengths and opportunities, clarifying the values that define how you behave and make decisions. You've defined the purpose and path that motivate your daily life while you are moving toward your aspirations. The following graph describes how you are strengthening your visionary mind.

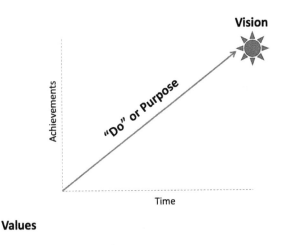

Figure 5: Do or Purpose

As you can see, the image you have of your future gives clarity to your whole being. It is a continuous exploration of what you want and who you are. How would you know your challenges and priorities if you don't really know what you want? That is where the frontal cortex in your brain starts analyzing your situation. Remember, you are the expert on your life and your own challenges. A professional coach is a very useful resource during this future creation process, for several reasons:

- To expand your thinking and empower yourself to look for options and possibilities.
- To allow you to explore more deeply what is meaningful for you and from there habituate you to create plans, make certain decisions, and let you find your inner motivation to execute your priorities.
- To facilitate the creation of your action plans.
- To make sure you are putting your time and effort toward continuously walking your own Do.
- To be a sounding board and confront you, and to help you catch yourself when you are going through a shortcut that is not benefiting the achievement of your goals.
- To empower you to open lines of communication with the people you will learn from most.

A professional coach will empower you to clarify your desired future by asking you powerful questions that make you think, introspect, and realize where you want to put your time and effort. A coach is a thinking partner for your development process to build your capability to achieve your vision. It is an experiential process driven by data from multiple perspectives and based on mutual trust and respect. As a result, you will create action plans to move past obstacles and achieve what you choose. I am mentioning a professional coach because I have seen the effectiveness of coaching over the last decade. You can boost your visionary mind at any time. Just be aware of what you really want and do what is relevant for your vision to continue making progress in your life and consequently in others' lives.

Often people around us try to help by providing advice we didn't ask for. Be aware that even when their intentions are good, they can bias the direction of what truly matters to you. Make sure you create your own future and develop the skills you require to overcome your own challenges to make it real. There are many people out there willing to empower you, willing to listen to you and ask you those tough questions that you must answer. Make sure that you are thoroughly exploring what you want for your future and what is relevant for you. Questions unlock opportunities. When you answer meaningful questions and imagine your future in detail, you free your visionary mind.

Your PSC: 4. Vision

Your *vision of the future* sets the direction of all your efforts. Make sure your vision feeds your soul. Be ready to answer the following questions that will open opportunities to create the future you really want. There are as many options as the universe has stars. Continue focusing on your visionary mind.

Now is the time to use all your imagination to picture that bright future that you will make happen in the next years to come, usually in five years or more.

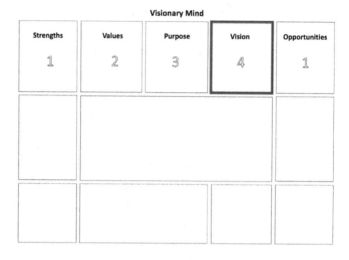

Figure 6: Vision

NINTH DAILY CHALLENGE

Here is when you use all your senses to imagine how your life will be a long time from now. It is a valuable exercise to free your mind. Write in your notebook or on a blank piece of paper all the ideas you have in mind about the future you will create. Expand your thinking and put yourself in a playful mode. Be as specific as you can—paint a picture, assemble a collage, or draw a mind map with all those ideas. To draw a mind map, draw a circle and in the center write the words "My Vision for 20XX." Write and connect with lines all the ideas about your future. You can also write or record the answers to the following questions. Most importantly, avoid judging or criticizing your thoughts.

Imagine seeing through time into the year 20XX:

- Where are you?
- How are you? Be very specific.
- Who is with you?
- What are you doing?
- What are you seeing, hearing, tasting, smelling, and touching?
- What are you feeling emotionally?
- What makes this reality inspiring and meaningful?

Make it vivid. Add as much detail as you can. Write or speak in first person and in present tense. It all starts with this dream, something you imagined, something you strongly believe. There are no limits—focus on the horizon you can see, the sounds you hear, the fragrances you smell, the flavors you taste, and of course, the sensations you feel. The more you recreate a detailed image, the more vivid and useful it will be. Your vision is your "north" to make sure you are walking your path in the right direction. You can adjust it and clarify some of the details, but as in a compass, north is always north. When you walk your path, there are times you might feel lost. Just review what you have just created: your values, your purpose, and your vision. It will give you the clarity of your direction.

To create your vision statement, I recommend you set what you want to accomplish in five years or more but not less. If you set a vision for one year, you may be talking about a short-term goal (three years is a medium-term goal, and five years a long-term goal). This is a long-term vision, not a short-term goal. Once you define the year, it must be written in first person and it must be written in present tense. In that way you are making it real and tying it to deep emotions. The importance of establishing the year by which to accomplish it is that it will show you how much you are progressing and give you a point of reference in time.

Now that you have explored and connected with your meaningful dreams, you are ready to summarize it using thirty-five words at the most. Yes, I know! This is the real challenge. In that way, you will be able keep just what is more relevant, and it will be easier to remember it as your north in life. Even though is very profound, it must be simple to be useful.

Examples of a vision statement for 20XX:

- I'm a recognized professional and a lovely husband with two kids whom I spend quality time with.
- I'm healthy and have an exemplary international network of valuable people who continuously support each other.

We usually go through life showing something different than who we are and what we really want. Be authentically you. Take off all you don't need, feel lighter, and enjoy the path to achieve your highest dreams. Live your personal Do and reach your dreams!

Patience is the essential quality of a man.

—Kwai-Koo-Tsu, from *Zen in the Martial Arts*
by Joe Hyams

Step Five: Weaknesses and Threats

Control your emotion or it will control you.

—Chinese adage

Turn Defeat into Success

We learn from our successes, but we learn far more from our mistakes and flaws. When I was a kid, I had an explosive character. From one perspective, that was good because when other kids were bothering me, I had the guts to stop them. From another perspective, that mindset was just serving my ego and my need to prove my strength. Most of the time, being explosive did not serve me or others. I had to learn how to respect myself and others by calming down my emotions and being one with conflict. After years of practice, I'm better but still have a long way to continue improving.

When I was in elementary school, a kid bothered me for days. So it happened that we got into a fight. The school gave me a report with a day and time listed for my parents to meet with the school's social worker. When I gave the report to my mom, she had a conversation with me that I recall very well.

At first, she was mad. Then she looked at me with lovely eyes and asked, "What happened? Tell me the truth, and I will support you as long as you weren't the one who started the fight."

Fortunately for me, I didn't start the fight, so I shared what happened.

Then she said with great seriousness, "Tell me the truth. I will not joke around with them. You better tell me everything. Because if you are hiding something and I find out later, you will be in deep trouble."

I explained exactly what happened. I was just defending myself.

Then she smiled and said, "I'm proud of you. Never let anyone take advantage of you. I will go to your school as many times as necessary if you are defending yourself."

Then she changed her tone, "But if you start a fight, or if I find out someone is hitting you and you are not telling the teacher or defending yourself, I will kick your butt."

I kind of understood but was also confused. On one hand, it was OK to be in a fight if I was defending myself. In fact, if I did nothing under those circumstances and my mom found out, I would be in trouble. On the other hand, I knew it was not good to be involved in a fight.

That time, the school's social worker, my mom, and the other kid's mom discussed what happened, and we both promised it would not happen again.

My karatedo sensei had taught me that a fight is the last recourse and usually doesn't resolve a situation. When I was younger, I had too many emotions flying like butterflies in my daily interactions. I wanted to be active all the time. My mind was always thinking. I had too much energy, and I knew there was something tantalizing about someone bothering me. Inside of me, I wanted to hit back because I wanted to have that adrenaline shot. But I knew I would have to have a very strong argument to at least say, "I didn't start the fight." I was having all those emotions and knew I must treat others with camaraderie and respect.

Fortunately, I was in a discipline where I could express that honorability and at the same time have the adrenaline of a fight in a controlled environment. When I was in elementary school, I had at least two opportunities during the week to be me, to be that thunder and that peace under the storm. A place where it was good to kick, punch, shout, and liberate all that energy from my body was my karatedo classes.

Years later, when I was seventeen years old, I had an argument with a bus driver. He was going to punch me, and without even realizing it, I knocked him out. It happened fast, and I didn't even think about it. It just happened. I was young, and I didn't really know the power I had developed.

It seemed I didn't learn the lesson that time. A year later, life gave me another chance to better handle a similar situation. This time I had to learn the lesson a rougher way. After dinner with Sensei Belmont, I was in a traffic jam on my way home when a taxi driver crashed into my car. It was a not a big deal for me—he was driving a little yellow Volkswagen Beetle, and I was driving an old red American Rambler (model year 1981, my first car—I loved it). This is relevant because his car was damaged, and mine just got a scratch. However, he crashed into me while I was not moving, so I thought it was going to be a simple conversation.

Unfortunately, when he approached, he did not seem friendly and did not show any willingness to talk. He just started blaming me. I was going to explain my perspective when I saw a slap coming to my face. I stepped back, but his fingers still hit my cheek. That started the fight, and this one was not as fast as the previous one. This time it lasted a few minutes. He was bigger than me and looked stronger. Unfortunately, I was afraid and was not thinking. I was just doing what my body was trained to do.

In the end, I broke his nose and jaw. When he said, "Please stop," I realized what just happened and that I was not hurt. The people who saw it may say I won. On the contrary, I felt I failed. I was already a karatedo black belt yet couldn't control myself. I was embarrassed. A policeman approached, and I saw a man explaining to him that I was defending myself. The policeman was evaluating the situation, and at that precise moment, the taxi driver was leaving. He looked at me and asked, "Are you OK?" I nodded. But I was not OK. My body was fine, but my emotions were everywhere. I felt like a failure. I felt sad, felt like I lost control. I only "won" because I was trained. But what upset me most was that I hit him so hard because I was afraid. He was older and bigger, and that idea blocked my mind. I realized I did not just lose control but also had no clue about how to solve the conflict without striking him.

When I arrived home, I called my sensei and apologized. I explained he punched me first, and I was afraid.

He said, "I'm glad you are OK. Did you break his leg or arm?"

I said, "No."

He said, "Good. He will be able to continue working and move on with his life tomorrow. He was trying to take advantage of you. He was older and bigger, and he thought he had an advantage over you. If he could have, he probably would have really hurt you.

"Now you know the responsibility you have. You are a white weapon, so use yourself wisely. It seems that you are finally grasping it: The real challenge and mastery is to win without fighting."

It has taken me many years to control that stampede of horses inside of my body, that instinct to go with the most primitive part of my being. Having learned not to react during risky situations unless there is a real threat has kept me out of trouble many times. I believe the awareness of my emotions to consciously seek calm has been one of my biggest challenges. I have had situations in my life in which I gave my best effort, but I know I still could have handled them better. Yet that self-control and self-discipline have shaped my character.

What I have learned training in karatedo, aikido, and iaido is how difficult it is to control the most primitive part of my being. It also has taught me that practice and having a clear intention in everything I do make self-control and self-mastery easier. I strongly believe self-mastery is accessible to anyone who decides to practice consistently. It is possible when you persevere in training and when you have a very clear outcome in mind in situations where instinct is taking over. It's about calming your mind and being one with the situation. If you think about it, there are no problems, just situations that are eager to be solved, that are looking for our attention so they can serve our path for self-growth.

When you understand you are your biggest enemy, when you make the decision to train yourself into a weapon to fight your weaknesses, a new phase in your life starts: a phase of self-knowledge and self-mastery to serve your own purpose. A way to better serve others. Our brains were created for survival, and in any situation, a brain is looking for the shortcut, a path it already knows. That's one reason it's so complicated to nurture new habits—we must program our brains with the new shortcut. For example, we need to shift from a negative mindset to a positive mindset, from feeling like the victim to becoming part of the solution, from being passive or aggressive to being assertive. We tend to take the shortcut because other paths seem too dangerous, risky, or full of traps. But if we change our mindset, they can be fun!

Training a new path will better serve your self-development, and the greatest news is that once you commit to it, you will grow and move forward, and no one can take that away from you. Use your growth mindset to live outside your comfort zone, where there are both risks and nice surprises. A lot of times I heard, "I'm too small compared to so-and-so," "I'm very behind compared to so-and-so," "I want to be like so-and-so," or "It's a long way to achieve what so-and-so achieved during that period." Do yourself a favor and stop. Focus all that energy on finding your own weaknesses and threats. Then wisely choose the ones you will improve to better serve your visionary mind (values, purpose, and vision).

Feed Your Mind and Spirit

Now, just imagine the value of openly asking people close to you, "What do you recommend I improve?" Would they answer with honesty and candor? It all depends on the trust, confidence, and respect you have built with each one. Even with trust, that person may not answer because, let's be real, who asks that? A person like you, a person who is growing and committed to self-mastery. A brave and courageous person with the humility to openly listen without judging or criticizing asks questions like that. A person like you who wants to learn from others, even about yourself, will. How much are you open to hearing others' points of view about you?

It's one thing to explore and know yourself through your eyes, and another thing to know yourself through the eyes of others. Just be honest with yourself. You are awesome. You are unique. Are you ready to embrace that journey? How much value will that information add to your life? How ready are you to receive that gift and simply thank them?

Leadership author Marshall Goldsmith introduced a concept called "feedforward," in which you let go of your ego, paradigms, and beliefs so you can see yourself through the eyes of others.[6] It's like being inside of a glass bottle, and the bottle has many name tags. You are wondering what they say. The solution is very easy: Just ask. Every question you ask about yourself to the people around you will uncover those name tags. The more accurate the question, the clearer it is to read it. You may read tags you don't like, that you believe don't belong to you. They do, at least from the perspective of each person.

Imagine a friend surprises you on a regular day. You are wondering about something in his hands. He is smiling and walking toward you.

As soon as he is close, he shakes your hand, gives you a hug, and says, "I saw this and thought about you. I really hope you enjoy it!"

Now you are excited. He said it in such a conclusive way that you accept it. Why not? It's a gift! You put it on your desk and open it. It is a yellow sweater—not yellow—it looks more like mustard! And what are those? They look like dots. You look closer and see that they are little salmon-colored ducks. You look at your friend, smile, and say, "Thank you!"

He smiles back and says, "I'm glad you like it."

You smile back, but deep in your mind you are thinking, *When am I going to use it?*

What happened there? In that specific scenario, you didn't like the gift. Some of you may be honest, laugh, and just share with him what bad taste he has. Let's imagine you were polite because you knew your friend had good intentions. What you appreciated was the gesture, the surprise, and the kindness. The gift is not relevant anymore; you can use it or not. That's your decision. There are going to be times you wear your gift, and there will be times that you just keep it for the right occasion; for example, an ugly sweater party to which your friend was not invited.

That's exactly what happens when you ask for others' perspectives. You are asking for their opinion (the gift). In the example, the gift was a surprise. Now think about the times that someone gave you their opinion without your asking. Surprise! Even when you ask, the content is unexpected, so it still has a surprise factor. When you are open to feedforward, there will be surprises. Some you may like. Sometimes you will feel neutral because probably you already knew, and sometimes it can be shocking. It requires training to accept it well.

Here is the tricky point: You can control how you receive the message—in this case, "the gift." What you can't control is how the other person will deliver the message. How will you deal with that? It depends on your self-mastery, related to your emotional intelligence. It depends where you are in your self-knowledge and your constant practice to get better. Your emotions can be triggered, but as in kumite, the more you practice, the more accustomed you will be to receiving feedforward and the more value you will get from that experience. If they see that you listen, you don't get defensive, and you use that information to adjust, they will continue to give you their perspective.

It requires courage, openness, self-control, acceptance, and humility. It also requires cutting your ego. These people are teaching you lessons. They are your senseis, even if they don't know it: They are mentoring you, and they know you well. Take advantage of all the gifts the people around you have to offer. Be mindful about whom to ask, and make sure you ask the people you are hesitating to ask. They are probably the ones you will learn from the most.

Often we are not open to exploring possibilities through the eyes of others because of the idea of right or wrong, the desire to be the smartest person in the room, and the story we tell ourselves. Feedforward is about opening up to possibilities, different perspectives, and seeing the world from different angles.

It is like a Rubik's cube. Imagine that you are in the street with people looking at a giant cube. You just see a blue wall with squares, and you are convinced it is blue because it is all that you can see. Then you look around and someone says it is also yellow, but you are seeing blue, so you don't believe it. That same person says, "I can prove it. Follow me." Then you turn the next corner and see a red wall, so you are convinced it's blue and red. Is it yellow, too? You continue walking and then turn the next corner. You realize it is yellow, too. After exploring all the different perspectives, all the different sides, you realize that you just had a little piece of reality, that life is much more complex.

A life situation might not be a Rubik's cube. It might be an irregular prism with many sides. At the end, it is the same prism. That prism is you. You can decide to stick to your point of view or explore different perspectives and accept them as a possibility. That's precisely the power of the concept of "parallel thinking," as coined by psychologist and writer Edward de Bono in his book *The Six Thinking Hats*.[7] You have to be open to different possibilities and different ways to see reality that are not necessarily through your eyes. The perspective from the people who know you well is a gift when they decide to share it with you. It is in your hands to create an open environment for success where you freely share perspectives and use what you learn to progress in your self-mastery.

How you communicate with others shows your self-mastery as well as how you adjust your communication to add value. As a result of your self-mastery in communication, you will realize how many times you add more value when you are quiet and listen than when you talk. Your ability to actively listen defines your success and empowers the achievements of others. It shows your humility in knowing any perspective is valuable because you respect differences. It is understanding we all can add value from our unique angles, while focusing everybody's minds on the same goal. It is about asking more than telling. It is about a deep understanding that when you try to be the smartest person in the room, you block communication, creativity, and innovation.

Good communication is understanding that we are vulnerable at any moment, and it is precisely that vulnerability that makes us shine. Let go of the need to show others how much you are shining. When you are complete and shining from within, your environment and the people around you will shine, too!

Your PSC: 5. Weaknesses and Threats

Now that you have explored your strengths, opportunities, values, purpose, and vision, it is time to focus on the other side of your internal and external factors: weaknesses and threats. As explained before throughout the book, these aspects are not necessarily negative. They are *your greatest masters* and are crucial to your growth. Please see them as your very close friends who are telling you the truth. A good friend tells you the good, the bad, and the ugly without hesitation. A good friend is gentle with wording but also knows hiding the truth would limit your growth—you know your friend is sharing it to add value to your life. You can decide to use their perspective or not. Please look at weaknesses and threats from the same approach.

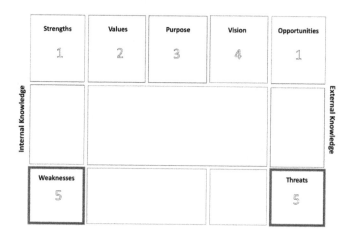

Figure 7: Weaknesses and Threats

Weaknesses

Your *weaknesses* are the opposite of your strengths, and both are internal (about yourself). The difference is that weaknesses teach you great lessons through life, if you are wise in choosing which weaknesses to address. This aspect is important because it is by far more effective to leverage all your efforts boosting your talents than improving your weaknesses. On the other hand, when you wisely choose a few weaknesses to focus on, it will open new paths for success. It means your self-awareness and discipline will go beyond what you are good at. You'll also create new strengths over time, which is awesome and over the years will expand your potential. Your weaknesses teach you lessons when you are aware and humble enough to accept them. We can either accept them or not and decide to do something about them or not. The bottom line is not to be perfect, but to make sure every day you are learning the lessons to be a better person tomorrow and the day after. This continuum never ends. It is about making peace with who you are, learning from it, and having a very clear idea of who you want to become. You may be very happy with your current reality, or you may not. The point here is knowing how you want to continue growing. When you worked on your strengths and opportunities during the first step of your PSC, you also started exploring about how other people perceive you. You are the expert of your own reality and challenges; now you know the way you look at yourself is not necessarily the way others look at you.

As we discussed previously, self-mastery is a contact sport, and one way to look at your weaknesses, aside from your own perspective, is through the eyes of others. Learn about yourself from different perspectives, and make it a habit for your self-growth. Your flaws and challenges are your great masters to become the greatest version of yourself.

TENTH DAILY CHALLENGE

Most of the time, instinct is not aligned with your purpose. The purpose you created previously can cool down your emotions and neutralize the eagerness to react. Sounds easy, but it requires lots of practice. A great way to focus your mind when your instincts start to take over is to stop and ask yourself:

- What is my purpose?
- What do I want to achieve?
- What will be the consequences of just reacting?
- What are the outcomes that I want to create?

It is about training your willingness to get better at something that you know will serve your goals. It is challenging but so rewarding. Through the years, you will be able to discipline your mind to act and not react. That doesn't mean you will not make mistakes.

We are humans—we fall, we stand up, and we continue making progress.

Create a list of weaknesses you believe you have using the following questions:

- What do I want to change about me?
- What changes can dramatically improve my life?
- What adjustments do I want to make?

With all that information in mind, write your biggest weaknesses. Start with the ones that once you improve them, would have the most positive impact in your results (a minimum of three and a maximum of seven). Then make sure you prioritize from the ones you want to improve that have the highest impact to the ones with least impact. Your focus will be on the most important weaknesses, the ones that will be a game changer in your life.

Examples of weaknesses are distant, explosive, too logical, abrupt, need to listen more, need to talk less.

ELEVENTH DAILY CHALLENGE

Every week, you are often interacting with the same people. Some people know you more than you realize. During this learning process, they can teach you great lessons. Just ask, be open, and practice your active listening. They will open the door for self-growth to continue progressing in your self-mastery. To continue feeding your mind and spirit, ask the following questions to your closest circle of influence (family, friends, colleagues, subordinates, clients, suppliers, bosses, etc.):

1. What am I doing well?
2. What can I do differently?
3. To be a better (leader, boss, dad, mom, colleague, friend, you name it), what do you recommend I improve?

Remember to ask the question, be silent, listen, and appreciate their candor and honesty. No matter what they said, whether you liked their answer or not, just smile and say thank you.

You will learn far more about your flaws from the people around you than anywhere else. You are opening a door, so make sure you maintain trust and openness over time, so they keep sharing their perspective. If you use what you consider valuable and adjust based on it, you will grow.

Little tips:

- Make sure you are friendly and naturally smiling.
- Ask the question and wait for the answer (make peace with silence).
- If you want to know more on each question, just ask, "What else?" Ask it repeatedly until they run out of ideas.

- Make sure your body language is receptive, arms visible and open (on the table or where you can place them comfortably), back straight, gestures gentle. If it is a phone call, naturally smile and listen actively.
- Take notes or really remember the conversation because it is valuable information for your self-analysis and to decide how will you use that information.
- Be authentic and say thank you!

This simple process will make a profound difference in your life, especially if you commit to use the information and come back to each person occasionally to explore if they are perceiving progress. You will be adjusting what makes sense based on the gift you are receiving. Share what you are working on and ask:

- What have you noticed?
- What do you recommend for me?

This exercise of learning about yourself from another's perspective, appreciating the gift, and adjusting accordingly will open amazing opportunities in your life. At the moment that you decide to make it a life challenge, you will be on your path and progressing in your self-mastery.

Threats

Threats are external factors that may block your progress and many times are situations that are out of your control or seem to be. The value of thinking about them is that they let you create contingency plans to be ready for challenges. Even when you believe you don't have an influence on certain threats, you may impact them indirectly. There are some variables you may not have an influence on but others you do. Think about your situation and the factors around you that may affect your plans (macroeconomics, politics, competition, trends, etc.).

TWELFTH DAILY CHALLENGE

Start writing a list of threats, using the following questions as guidance:

- What may block my ability to achieve what I want?
- What is happening that may impede my progress?
- What could happen that might affect me?

Focus on the ones with the highest probability; write a minimum of three and a maximum of seven. Your first three must be the top threats you will focus on neutralizing.

Example of threats are change of government, volatile exchange rate, and growth of competition.

It's about disciplined thinking to promote the emotions to guide you toward the life you want. It's a question of deliberate practice. It's about building your character, nurturing your self-improvement, and building winning relationships. It's about facing a deep understanding of yourself and those around you.

For the uncontrolled there is no wisdom, nor for the uncontrolled is there the power of concentration; and for him without concentration there is no peace. And for the unpeaceful, how can there be happiness?

—The Bhagavad Gita

Step Six: Internal Goals

Nature does not hurry, yet everything is accomplished.

—Lao Tzu

Choose Your Battles

Everything starts with yourself. If you passively wait for things to happen, very likely you will finish disappointed. As shared before, it is about practice, boosting your strengths, and deciding where to focus. Your vision is giving the overall direction, and your goals are contributing to its achievement. Therefore, they must be aligned with your "north," like having some metal scrap on a table and then placing a magnet to align everything to the same direction. It is not possible to grow in all directions at the same time. Therefore, you must choose your battles, which goals you will achieve. Your goals must contribute to your visionary mind. You are getting better at the art of balancing your strengths and weaknesses. Too much strength, and you will get stiff. Too much weakness may limit your progress.

It is about flowing and adjusting. We all know the importance of goal-setting. Start imagining you are building a ladder one step at a time. After a while, when you look back, you will feel proud of yourself. You will feel proud of your achievements because you are climbing your own ladder. You are doing it in such a way that you are enjoying the view, the feeling of your legs, the air you are inhaling and exhaling. Break down your goals in tiny steps in a plan with a clear idea of the future you are creating. Be flexible to adjust it and iterate all the times necessary, and most importantly, love the trip. Once the goal is clear, the focus is in your personal Do. Make it an enjoyable one.

Make peace with your personal Do. We all have parameters, and our ego is looking for a continuous comparison. We tend to look at what other people have achieved by a certain age or during a certain amount of time. We all advance at different paces and under different circumstances. Any time is a good time to start. It is not about them; it is about you. It is about your process, your life, your goals. You are building the sequence of your own events that is shaping your own history. Some people look at others through their own lenses of what success looks like, and most of the time, they start emulating that success, emulating others' goals. The problem with that approach is that disappointment and anxiety may grow. On the other hand, when you commit to a similar path and customize it to make it your own, you will find new ways to ensure the achievement of your goals.

Be authentic with your goals. It's your path, your trip. You are creating it, and you have company. You have a choice, and it's in your hands to make it a reality. Understanding what you want and the reason you want it will be the fuel for the achievement of each one of your goals. When you tie your goals to your values, purpose, and vision, you are expanding your inner motivation to accomplish it. It is all about finding the way to increase your well-being by achieving what you want and really enjoying your path.

THIRTEENTH DAILY CHALLENGE

You have all the answers. Just start your own adventure. Start creating each one of your goals. Explore at what pace you want to walk your path and explore:

- What are your goals?
- Who has walked a similar path before?
- Who has been part of your path?
- Who will be part of your path in the future?

Review what you have in your PSC and use all that information to prioritize your goals.
You are ready. Choose your battles!

Your PSC: 6. Internal Goals

Goals give you clarity about your future. The biggest benefit is not achieving your goal but what you focus on and the person you become while pursuing your goal. Before creating your goals, *analyze and evaluate your current situation.* Reflection makes your goals more effective and is one reason writing your goals is the sixth step on your PSC. Before starting, review again your strategic elements (vision, purpose, values, strengths, opportunities, weaknesses, and threats) and adjust them if needed.

Your internal goals come from reflecting on your strengths and weaknesses. Now that you are certain about the previous aspects of your PSC, it is time to write down your dreams and turn them into goals.

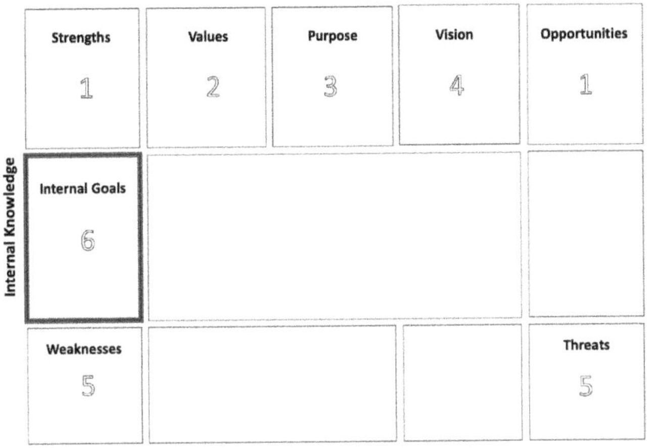

Figure 8: Internal Goals

FOURTEENTH DAILY CHALLENGE

The following questions will be helpful during this process. Be specific enough so you will know when you will accomplish each one of them.

- Analyze your strengths and choose the ones you will boost this year.
- Analyze your weaknesses and choose the ones that you decide to improve.
- What do I want (at a personal, professional, or any other level)?
- What else? (Ask many times until you run out of ideas.)
- How will those goals serve my purpose?
- What do I want to adjust?
- When do I want to have each one of them done? It can be short-term (one year), medium-term (two to three years), or long-term (four to five years).
- After I accomplish them, what will I see/hear/feel/taste/smell?

What you are writing is providing you focus. It is shaping your dreams, and it is giving you the ability to narrow down the actions you need to achieve whatever you want in life. Your notes right now are a great tool but probably are not written in the most effective way to have a powerful goal. To be powerful, it must cause you to stretch and grow in ways you never have before.

SMART Goals

Almost four decades ago, Professor George T. Doran introduced us to the concept of SMART goals, that is, goals that are Specific, Measurable, Assignable, Realistic, and Time-Related.[8] I've seen it work for our clients. The approach I take to SMART goals comes from sharing perspectives with colleagues and friends in the training and development industry. We will discover each aspect one by one.

Specific

When setting a goal, it must be understandable to any person reading it. Even if you are the only one who will read it, being specific gives you clarity on exactly what it means to complete that goal. In addition, it makes it easier to define the steps to achieve it.

Goal: I want to visit Japan.

Specific goal: I want to visit Kyoto and Osaka to train and polish my martial arts skills.

Measurable

Your goal must show how will you measure progress or success. Some people set goals as ideas to work on in the future, which is good. The next step is to make sure you find a way to set a metric to monitor your progress through time.

Measurable goal: I want to visit Kyoto and Osaka to polish my martial arts skills during seven full days of training.

Actionable

To set a powerful goal, it must have action verbs and a language that motivates you to work on them. The words you use and the tone of the goal will have an impact on how you perceive it, your emotions, and your results.

The original model uses the word *assignable* to specify who will do it, and other frameworks use the word *attainable*. In your PSC, it is clear that you are the one accountable for making it happen. The reason I don't recommend using the word *attainable* is because it may limit the goal. What is not considered attainable by one person may be considered attainable by another. What really defines attainability are the steps, the action plan, any people involved, the quality of the coordination and leadership of those efforts, and the amount of time allotted for planning and execution.

Of course, it is important to have your feet on the ground. At the same time, feel free to dream high if you are willing to put in all the intelligence, effort, and time to achieve it. Many people in history achieved what the world said was impossible. Remember that whatever you believe is possible or not, you're right!

Actionable goal: I will visit Kyoto and Osaka to polish my martial arts skills during seven full days of training at the World Premier Olympics of Japanese Traditional Budo.

Relevant

Many times, a goal is written on a piece of paper or lies just in the mind of its creator. Your goal must be relevant and aligned with your highest priorities: values, purpose, and vision (your visionary mind). We are changing all the time, and the initial goal may evolve to something very different from its original root. Make sure to keep it aligned with your visionary mind. The relevance of your goal will make follow-through easier. It is vital to write it down and create a way to keep track of it and its evolution. Your PSC is a great tool to have everything visible on the same page. In addition, it is smart to create a system to monitor it. It could be a spreadsheet, a mind map, a file in your computer, or any medium to help you see it, feel it, or even hear it. Many free apps and software may help you with that. Be mindful about the relevance of your goals and how you will keep track of the evolution of your goals, with a very clear idea of what you will achieve. Other frameworks use the word *realistic,* and the reason why I don't recommend it is similar to what I explained before about the use of *attainable.*

> **Relevant goal:** I will visit Kyoto and Osaka to polish my spirit and martial arts skills and continue progressing in my self-growth during seven full

days of training at the World Premier Olympics of Japanese Traditional Budo in the commemorative year of 2020.

Time-Oriented

Finally, a concept that is key and many times is omitted is setting a deadline. Review your current situation and set a deadline, considering life happens. Be real about your bandwidth and the changes you will make to have the time to work on them. How proficient are you with disciplining yourself to focus on your priorities? Remember that unplanned things can happen (an accident, illness, another project, etc.). If it is a real priority, you will make it happen, and even in that situation, consider a cushion of time for unplanned events. When setting a deadline, be specific. For example, instead of writing "at the end of the year," say "before December 15." The more specific and real, the more it will guide your daily decision-making.

> **Time-Oriented goal:** I will visit Kyoto and Osaka from April 17 to May 9, 2020, to polish my spirit and martial arts skills and continue progressing in my self-growth during seven full days of training at the World Premier Olympics of Japanese Traditional Budo in the commemorative year of 2020.

As mentioned before, your internal goals are related to your strengths and weaknesses. An internal goal is tied to your habits, attitudes, feelings, and any other characteristic of your uniqueness. In the next chapter we will uncover external goals, which are related to environmental factors, with our opportunities and threats. Review one more time the example I provided for the SMART goal. That example is an external goal because it is considering the interaction with my surroundings and factors on which I may have limited control. You have full control of your internal goals; they are all about who you are.

Think thoroughly about your short-term (one year) goals. Save the medium- (two to three years) and long-term (four to five years) goals for later. By the way, the example I wrote was originally an external long-term goal when I was invited to participate in the event in 2016. Now it is a short-term goal that will happen within a year, so I have added it to my PSC.

Write down your internal short-term goals and choose the most important one to three goals, the ones that will create a quantum leap in your results. Then make them SMART. Have in mind that you are creating your internal goals based on the strengths and weaknesses you have chosen to focus on.

Examples of internal goals:

- "Share my ideas only when I'm adding value and ask my colleagues once a month about my progress in improving my communication skills."

- "Work on the priorities I set in my agenda during the first two working hours each day to achieve meaningful daily results before noon."
- "Practice positive thinking, rate my progress on a scale from one to ten every Friday, and once a month ask those around me whether they've noticed improvement."

Once your goals are clear, build a plan, create your path, and flow with it. It sounds logical and simple but requires the development of new habits that will nurture your life. Now that you are certain about your top three internal goals, your execution and progress will be easier.

You will achieve all your dreams. Just decide to do everything in your hands to become better!

It doesn't matter how slowly you go, so long as you do not stop.

—Confucius

Step Seven: External Goals

When the student is ready, the Master appears.

—Buddhist proverb

Teachers Are Learners

Ateacher is someone who shares lessons or guides by example because of their experience. We can even learn from people who don't consider themselves teachers. Someone may inspire us to move forward and, on some occasions, become our mentor even without noticing.

In Japan, such a person is called a *sensei*. The word comes from *sen* (before or precedence), and *sei* (life, genuine, or birth), literally meaning "a person born before another." This concept comes from the understanding that all people born earlier often have more experience to share with others in a given discipline or skill.

In traditional budo, a sensei is not only a teacher but an honorable guide for helping the students become their better selves. The sensei helps them to accomplish what they want in life, to build valuable skills such as focus, discipline, perseverance, respect, honorability, calmness, and inner peace.

A traditional budo sensei uses the "martial way" (as opposed to calligraphy or tea making) as the path to those deeper attributes. A sensei is someone who has been in the path of self-development and enlightenment longer than others. They have been continuously training their mind, body, and spirit to become a living example of their teachings. Their actions and behavior, not their words and promises, demonstrate congruency. Humility is key for learning and key for teaching. A sensei knows during every second of every single class they themselves have many things to learn. The students are a key part of the virtuous cycle of teaching, practicing, failing, succeeding, and continuous learning.

In budo, *sensei* is a term given by others, not a term given by the person themselves. In other words, many people are called teachers, but just a few are titled "Sensei."

Many years ago, I started training a five-year-old named Diego. After many years of karatedo, he became *shodan*, or first-rank black belt, at age thirteen. He reached the point where he was ready to start his path as an instructor. I had a conversation with him and his parents, and we all agreed he was going to teach the kids' karate class. There was just one little detail: He was only fifteen years old. But he was mentally ready and mature enough to become a great sensei.

I had a conversation with Porfirio, another of my advanced students, who was one rank below black belt. Porfirio had his bachelor's degree and was twenty-seven years old. I told him Diego was ready to lead the kids' class and that it would be great if he could team up with Diego as a *senpai*, an advanced and trusted student who supports the sensei. Porfirio immediately agreed and was even grateful for the opportunity to serve. This is what I mean when I talk about values and nurturing an environment of traditional budo. Porfirio didn't even remark that he was older than Diego. There was no ego involved. He just knew that Diego was in charge because Diego was "born" earlier in karatedo than he. To this day, they continue training and collaborating with camaraderie and respect. No one is more or less than anyone. They are in their own path of getting better, not anyone else's. Their competition is against themselves.

We are all learners, and we all have something to share. It is inspiring to think that even teachers have teachers. We are all beginners—it is just that some of us have been beginners longer. I have been with people who believe knowledge and experience come from older people. In a way, they think age gives the right to give a valuable opinion. But we can all give a valuable opinion because we are all humans, and humans are smart. Experience certainly has a high specific weight, but humility, openness, consistency, and congruency are by far more valuable than all the experience in the world without those attributes. Those attributes are the real engine of growth. It is much more important how we think, behave, analyze, adjust, and continually improve over time. It starts with each one of us on a foundation of honor and personal accountability.

The World Is Your Sensei

We can be open to learning from anywhere—from nature, a little kid, an animal, or an insect. Mother Nature speaks to us every day, starting with what our bodies are feeling and "saying." When we look at the sky, the ocean, and the forest, we can be aware of opportunities, be open to hear, see, taste, smell, and touch new experiences. We have just a tiny piece of information, limited experiences that shape who we are and how we think. What we believe we know is just a piece of an infinite puzzle of different perspectives. Any time we think we are right, we need to remember that the real value resides in the respect, acceptance, and conjunction of all perspectives.

None of us has the right answer. We are full of our points of view and knowledge from our specific backgrounds, education, and family. We are culturally charged, depending on our experiences growing up. Learning goes beyond tolerance of other ideas. When a perspective is not harmful, it is worthy of us seeking to learn from it and expand our sight and our world.

The greatest sensei of your life is . . . yourself! How are you connecting with your inner self? How often are you spending time with nature? Are you understanding your surroundings? Do you take time to understand the world and how to take care of it? How much are you letting the world teach you? Open yourself to possibilities and create space for new experiences. The world is full of wisdom. How open are you to letting a bonfire, the ocean, the stars, or a landscape put you in a meditation mode? Peacefully think, feel, and sense your possibilities. Clarify what you want based on your opportunities and threats. Focus your time and effort to live a memorable life, a life on your own terms. Courage and humility make it possible to learn a lesson from anyone. How ready are you to give and receive what the world has to offer? How can you get ready to say, "I can learn from any situation. I will grow in harmony with the world; the world is my sensei"?

Your PSC: 7. External Goals

Most of what I explained in internal goals applies to external goals. Start by analyzing and evaluating your current situation. Then create your external SMART goals. The difference from your internal goals is that your external goals are considering your environment and are based on your opportunities and threats. This introspection opens new channels of thinking and doing. Life is designed for us to dream for the future and live in the present. The present can have many difficult obstacles, so setting goals provides long-term vision. Review again your vision, purpose, and values. They must give you a sense of belonging. They must represent you. As your internal goals are related to attitudes, habits, and behaviors to move forward toward your vision, your external goals are related to opportunities you will take advantage of to overcome potential threats.

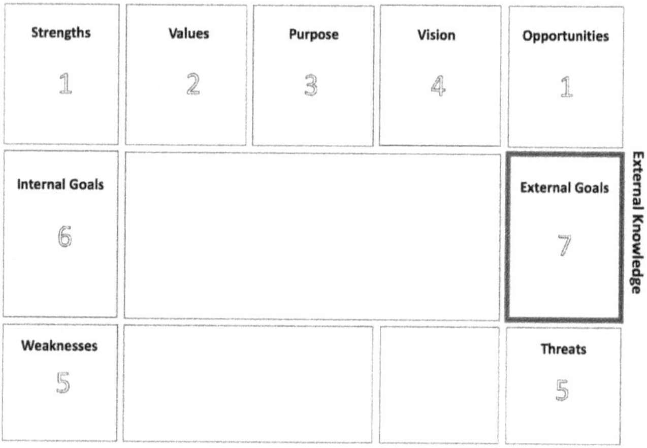

Figure 9: External Goals

Create goals for the short, medium, and long term. Generally, long-term goals guide short-term goals to overcome our current obstacles. For now, your PSC will have just your one-year goals. How you choose to prioritize is key for success. If you choose too many priorities, you won't have any priorities at all. Write all your ideas down, set a deadline, focus on your short-term goals (within the next twelve months), and choose the top three with the highest impact and the biggest ROTE (Return on Your Time and Effort). Then polish them and make sure they are SMART.

FIFTEENTH DAILY CHALLENGE

Being aware of your environment is key to defining your external goals. Answer the following questions and be specific, taking into consideration the SMART goals discussed in the previous chapter.

- Analyze your opportunities and choose the ones you will take advantage of this year.
- Analyze your threats and choose the ones that may block the achievement of your vision.
- What do I want (at a personal, professional, or any other level)?
- How will those goals serve my purpose?
- What do I want to adjust?
- When do I want to have each one of them done? It can be short-term (one year), medium-term (two to three years), or long-term (four to five years).
- After I accomplish them, what will I see/hear/feel/taste/smell?

Analyze very well your surroundings and take the most advantage of what you can control or at least directly impact to some level.

Remember, to be SMART, your goal must be specific enough to give you clarity and focus. It must be measurable, to track your progress. It must be actionable, written with powerful words about how to practically achieve it and to keep you motivated. It must be relevant, so you can see how it contributes to the achievement of your vision, and it must have a specific length of time to get it done.

Examples of external goals:

- "Get my coaching certification before February 12."
- "Gain three new clients paying $4,000 per month each by November 30."
- "Sell $150,000 dollars with five clients by October 30."
- "Increase my close ratio to 37 percent."
- "Train myself and boost my team's talent by delegating 80 percent of my current functions by August 15."

Your goals set a direction and the distance to achieve it, like a vector. Now, you have the clarity of what to do, when to do it, and why you are doing it. How to achieve it is part of an action plan you will create later for each goal. Have in mind that you are creating your external goals based on your priorities related to your environment (opportunities and threats). Remember that the world is your sensei.

Teachers open the door, but you must enter by yourself.

—Chinese proverb

Step Eight: Affirmations

Flow with whatever may happen and let your mind be free: Stay centered by accepting whatever you are doing. This is the ultimate.

—Chuang-Tzu, Chinese philosopher
(Fourth century BC)

Practice and Flow

My body has changed, my mind has changed, and where my soul wants to go with the years is becoming clearer. It has been like layers of knowledge and understanding about my life. It's amazing how we better understand our surroundings when we better understand who we are. During the last few years, I've been realizing how everything changes—even things we don't want to change because they're lovely the way they are. Yet if everything else changes, what is the point of trying to stay still? We can set a direction, but to get there, we will have to swim sometimes, walk sometimes, run sometimes, hike, or even surf. Many times, we may not end up where we wanted to go. Sometimes the wave is just pointing a different direction, and acquiring new skills is crucial to surf the new wave.

Our brains have an amazing capacity to focus on what benefits our lives. They have the capacity to let go of what is not adding value, even if it is something we really like. Our minds can also focus on the advantages of the new situation, on the new learnings, lessons, and doors that are open now. They can home in on the adventure of starting new journeys and the joy to feel alive. The change may hurt, but you can enjoy it—yes, you read right! Today, you decide to feel the pain. Tomorrow, you will be back to your life and will retake control.

Pain can be beautiful because it makes good moments more enjoyable. The best moment to take control of your life and flow with it is now! It doesn't matter when you read this paragraph again. It will apply every single time. Even if the wave or the flow of the river makes you finish in a different place, you can always find your path. You may have to travel a long way until you are on track. It doesn't matter. It happens to all people; the only difference is that some people give up. Others haven't found their path, but for them, it is not important where the current is going. Some people feel happy with their situations.

When I think about all the experience I have gotten in my life, in business, and in budo, I feel amazed to see my progress. I could claim I did it effortlessly, but that is not true. I just had a very clear idea of what I wanted and felt passionate about. During the process, I have learned the skills to focus all my efforts on enjoying my personal Do. When you flow with your challenges, with your mind calm and with clarity of where you want to go, you will get closer every single day and eventually achieve what you want.

Practice flow in any environment you are in. You will need to build new skills and habits to grow as a person. The more we grow, the bigger the goals we will be able to achieve. Your tiny decisions day by day are the foundation to make the difference and change your life. Some people make big changes in their lives when they fall hard. That works, too, because the pain is unbearable, and you have no choice but to go up. There is nothing else below. But why wait until everything falls apart? Even though it works for some people, you'd be leaving yourself in a reactive mode. If you choose victimhood, those who could inspire you will be repelled, while those who also enjoy victimhood will be attracted to you. Act now and take responsibility for your actions. It is your life and your responsibility to adjust the direction. Avoid hitting rock bottom. Make a choice to take step one. The more you wait, the more it may take to get where you want to be. This concept has the potential to transform your life and therefore transform your environment. Transformation is acceptance of possibilities with action. Sometimes reality slaps us in the face because we didn't see it coming, decided not to pay attention, or decided not to act.

Focus, action, and repetition are requirements for deliberate practice. When you take full responsibility and commit to it, you will flow with your passions and dreams because you are immersed in the moment. A great way to keep you flowing is by using affirmations to focus your body, mind, and spirit toward what you really want in life. Continue reading, and you will discover key ideas for your success.

Tighten Your Efforts

In budo, we use a powerful concept called *kime* in Japanese: to tighten the mind. This concept has been with me almost all my life. It is about excluding any external thoughts that are not concerned with achieving your immediate goal. Once you know where you want to go, it is about not being concerned about the past or the future. The only thing relevant is this precise moment. Every moment must add value to your life. It is a decision you make at every moment. It is about focusing your mind, your body, and your spirit. In his book *Zen in the Martial Arts*, writer and martial artist Joe Hyams quotes Bruce Lee as saying, "In life as well as on the mat, an unfocused or 'loose' mind wastes energy."[9] How focused is your mind? A focused mind will lead to a focused body and to a focused spirit. Imagining yourself as water, you could use focus—or kime—to cut whatever material you want, like a high-pressure industrial waterjet tool. Similarly, focus your mind on a tiny area with great pressure—that is precisely the concept of kime. This concept in budo is vital. You may have seen a *karateka* kick, block, or punch with great speed, which at the end is like an explosion. Physically, that's a way to see kime in action. They are relaxing their muscles during the trajectory and at the precise moment of the impact, focusing their whole being on a specific spot. That martial artist is grabbing all that energy from the floor. Their stance is their foundation to flow all the energy through their body like a jet of water. At the moment of impact, their mind, abs, and all the muscles of their body tighten for an instant while shouting, "Kiai!" That shout comes from the guts, from the contraction of the abs at the precise moment of the impact. When punching, all the energy of their body is focusing just in the middle finger knuckle, not the whole fist. The goal is to focus all that energy in a little area with kime.

This concept also helps in situations where you think something is too hard or you are too tired. Kime focuses your mind to that continuous last effort. It requires practice, and physical practice is a great way to train it. One example is if a mom saw her child under a car and lifted the car. Once her kid was safe, she would probably faint. This scenario is extreme, and that's the point! It's a powerful concept with many biological mysteries behind it. Something very clear is that adrenaline gives a shot of extra energy.

In martial arts, we train our brains to be in that state of awareness, to be able to attack and be calm again right away. During a training, our body may be too tired and may be willing to give up. But our mind and spirit are shouting, "Kime!" We feel it with our blood, muscles, breath, our bare feet on the floor, the sweat on our fists. We constantly prove to ourselves that kime is present.

When I was younger, I trained a lot—almost eighteen hours per week. I loved the feeling of my body getting sore from the muscle effort, the impact of my knuckles on the *makiwara* (padded striking post used as a training tool), the impacts on my forearms and shins, and the kicks of my classmates on my abs. Part of the training was to build endurance, to be strong enough to resist a punch or kick if we couldn't block it. Every training was like that—even when I ran, it was focused on beating my time, while keeping my energy up.

Now, years later, I realize that kime can also hurt me if I continue training in the same way. For me to enjoy the training, I required a constant feeling of pain, a pain I liked, but still pain. Then it happened . . . my body was not young anymore, and I started to feel how my body was not able to recover like before. I wasn't as fast, and my reflexes were not like before. My mind got stronger, but my body started to get hurt more often. I started yoga and swimming to relax my muscles, stretch them, and really feel my body. I realized too much kime was hurting me. At yoga, I learned a deeper understanding of my muscles, even little ones that I didn't know were there. Class after class was a new discovery of my body, my balance, or another way to concentrate and flow. I was learning other ways to enjoy exercising. I was training, not to be ready for an attack or to be able to evade and counterattack—I was learning a new way of enjoying effort and listening to what my body had to say. It had *so* many things to say, like, "I'm not that young, so please be kind."

Kime now has to be with pushing my whole being further, not just my body. Pushing my whole being to be aware of my surroundings helps me avoid hurting myself or others. It is still about tightening my mind in everything I do, and at the end of the day, I can feel proud of my achievements. It's also about giving my best version of myself to others, making my words count by doing, not by saying. Sensei Belmont once told me, "Never let your mouth move faster than your kicks." I answered with "*Oss!*", an affirmation of the positive attitude, high spirits, and refusal to quit that all karatekas seek to develop as we train. Now I can say my kicks are not faster, higher, or more powerful than when I was in my twenties. Probably my body has a different performance in karate, a performance of someone who is getting older, just like all who live life. What really matters is who I am today. My mind and spirit are stronger than before. I know I must empower others and focus on the way I behave and perform in my daily routine, flowing with life. Sometimes by being water or by surfing the wave, I achieve more than I do trying to paddle against the flow. I have been practicing all my life, and I still have a way to go. Sometimes the river or the wave knocks me over. It is fine—that means I should continue flowing like water, learn new skills, or practice more.

It is my duty to show all these concepts to the people around me, so they can achieve better outcomes. They can benefit from them even if they never have been to a martial arts training. I really hope you honor my sensei's words and never let your words get ahead of your actions. You can even affirm to yourself, "My actions are naturally ahead of my words."

Your PSC: 8. Affirmations

Affirmations are about shaping the mind by repeating statements you wish to be true. With carefully crafted statements, you can shape the mind to go with the flow, practice consistently, and focus with the intensity of kime in pursuing your vision. This is a part of your Personal Strategy Canvas™ I know you will love, and it will be a great way to keep you focused. So far you have completed the horseshoe of your PSC:

- Your visionary mind
- Your internal knowledge
- Your external knowledge

The horseshoe is the foundation to start working on your execution and focus. This is a good moment to review one more time what you have created so far and make all the adjustments you want. You can create a beautiful PSC, but create a way to make it a reality, so it can also be a powerful one!

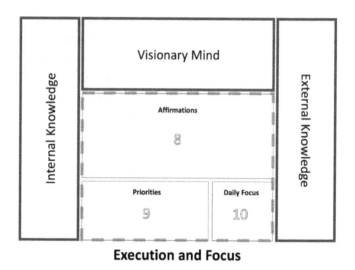

Execution and Focus

Figure 10: Execution and Focus

Look at your canvas and analyze everything you wrote. Make all the adjustments needed, and make sure it is describing your essence, what you truly are, and what you truly want. Now is the moment to use kime to tighten your body, mind, and spirit. Remember you will focus all your time and efforts like a waterjet tool. Many of your achievements will come from the compound effect of your daily decision-making second by second. Your affirmations will be your power tool for success.

You are creating your path, and you are the only one responsible for making it happen. Personal accountability is key to see your dreams come true, starting with the way you think and behave. Your discipline of thinking will lead you toward your ideal life and get you closer to the life you want. Be aware that some words limit your results, while others empower your results. For example, it is not the same to say, "I would like to give my best to act on my priorities and not procrastinate" and "I will act daily on my priorities and will focus on my results." The first one is open to possibilities, even to the possibility of failing. It is talking about doing instead of simply committing to action and also has the negative word "not." To make a statement powerful, you must say what you want, not what you do not want. The second statement is certain, precise, and shows 100 percent commitment to achieving the goal. Even more powerful is this:

"I am making progress regarding my priorities and creating daily results on time."

The difference is that the last one is in present tense, which makes it more real and gives you 100 percent accountability. If you hesitate about using that kind of language, please review your canvas again until it really represents who you are and who you want to become. The power of affirmations is to make you flow and focus your actions on your goals and highest priorities.

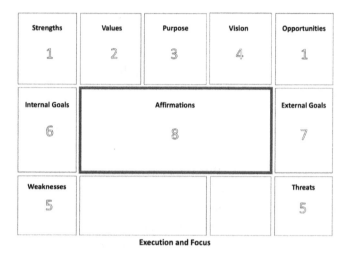

Figure 11: Affirmations

SIXTEENTH DAILY CHALLENGE

Follow these basic rules to create powerful affirmations:

- Brainstorm all the affirmations that come to your mind.
- Consolidate all of them in categories to avoid duplicates.
- Align them with your visionary mind and internal and external goals.
- Choose your top ten affirmations that will change your life.
- Create positive statements, using just positive words.

- Write in first person, expressing accountability.
- Write in present tense, making it real.
- Use empowering language and words that motivate you.

After writing them on your PSC, give a home to each affirmation. For example, write each affirmation on a sticky note and post it where it makes sense to you (the refrigerator, your wallet, your desktop, etc.). Be creative, use your imagination, and have them visible to focus your thoughts and your daily actions on that direction.

A powerful affirmation is a tool to keep you focused and working constantly in your top priorities. Your affirmations will empower your thoughts to nurture productive emotions and inspire you to act toward your results. For now, you will create up to ten affirmations based on your vision, internal goals, and external goals. Everything should be tied together as a system for your own success. We achieve results through execution, through committing to action. Anything else is good intentions, and intentions don't lead anywhere. Turn on the switch of change by writing affirmations in present tense, believing them, reading them, and continuously acting on them.

Examples of affirmations:

- "I enjoy every day and feel comfortable with new challenges."

- "I encourage my team and empower them to grow with a great attitude."
- "I discipline my thoughts and emotions to focus on solutions."
- "I feel amazing because I work out, eat healthfully, and sleep seven hours per day."

Remember to flow like water and to tighten your mind!

Empty your mind, be formless. Shapeless, like water.
If you put water into a cup, it becomes the cup.
You put water into a bottle, and it becomes the bottle.
You put it in a teapot, it becomes the teapot.
Now, water can flow, or it can crash.
Be water, my friend.

—Bruce Lee

Step Nine: Priorities

The sword has to be more than a simple weapon;
it has to be an answer to life's questions.

—Miyamoto Musashi, samurai and philosopher

Overcome Yourself

I n traditional budo or classical Japanese arts, we each train the body to become a weapon itself, but a weapon for what? Many people may think it is a weapon to fight against others, a common misunderstanding. Of course, a martial art must be effective self-defense. That's why it must be trained and mastered throughout the years. Yet in budo, we are certain the biggest enemy is oneself. We are the ones sabotaging our goals. We train with discipline to defend against ourselves and overcome our bad habits. As mentioned before, "karatedo" means "the way of the empty hand." We use our entire bodies to add value to everything we touch. It is about using the tools in our empty hands for good, for justice, to benefit others. We understand that as individuals, we can make a difference in our lives, and we can positively impact others to transform their lives and improve our society. We all can take part in the creation of a happier world, but we must choose our priorities and where we add the most value.

The real challenge in life is against oneself. Our environment and the people we know are just resources that we can take advantage of to continue growing. When the focus is on learning from each other, our opportunities are exponential. When we focus with all our beings on living our own Do, we make progress, and we naturally become a point of reference for others. The only battle to win is the one against oneself every single day. We all know what is good for us: exercising, eating healthily, resting well, balancing our lives, focusing on what is relevant, spending time with family and friends. We all know that by working on those priorities, we will have a richer life. But our minds and bodies play tricks on us. During the morning, we may feel so relaxed that it is easier to stay in bed than to get up and start stretching or working out. It's easier to eat fast food or eat a snack than to prepare a healthy meal. It's more fun to waste our time watching TV or on our cellphones, rather than go bed early at night. It's by far easier to work on something we enjoy than on the duties we know will serve better our purpose. It's by far easier to procrastinate and to say that we have too much work rather than balancing and organizing our work in such a way we can spend time with family and friends, have fun, and still complete all our commitments.

It's all about the habits that you create and how you sustain those habits. Start by managing yourself and choosing what to do with your time and effort. You can either waste your time or invest your time. The key is to have control over it. You are wasting your time when you are not getting value from the time spent. When you invest your time, you get something of value, such as learning a new skill, reading a book, or obtaining something that will nurture you. We all have time to waste or invest—the point is to have control of it and make a conscious decision. Start by managing yourself and having clarity about what really matters to you. When your priorities are clear, your decision-making is simpler and more effective. Of course, it requires discipline. To be disciplined means that you do whatever it takes at this moment to serve your purpose, even if you are not in the mood or you feel tired. You are disciplined when you are letting your being know who is in charge. When your purpose and meaning in life are in charge, it is easier to be disciplined and passionate.

Your PSC: 9. Priorities

Your affirmations are like a programming language to focus your being on your most important priorities. But it is not magic; it requires hard work, practice, and a very high level of self-awareness. If someone tells you that just because you write, read, and repeat affirmations, your life will improve, they are wrong. As we explored previously, if you read them, have them handy, record them, listen to them before going to sleep, and *act* on them, then of course, you will succeed because those affirmations are guiding your daily decision-making second by second. You are deciding to think differently, and those tiny decisions over time create a compound effect that will make a difference in your life and in the lives of the people around you.

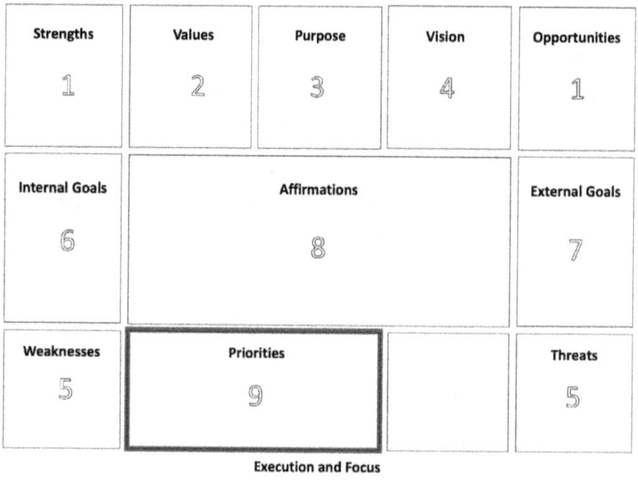

Strengths	Values	Purpose	Vision	Opportunities
1	2	3	4	1

Internal Goals	Affirmations		External Goals
6	8		7

Weaknesses	Priorities		Threats
5	9		5

Execution and Focus

Figure 12: Priorities

While your affirmations are key beliefs, your priorities are the key actions to focus your daily efforts to make them come true. Your priorities are the foundation to achieve extraordinary productivity. The effectiveness of your actions is completely dependent on your ability to differentiate the urgent from the important. Many people call this "time-management skills." I believe there is no such thing as time-management—we cannot change time or have an influence on it. The only thing you can do is learn to manage yourself. Instead of thinking you will manage your time, say things like this:

- "I will manage myself."
- "I will manage my priorities."
- "I will create a plan, stick to it, and flow with it."
- "I will honor my commitments."
- "I will be accountable and will make it happen."

There is a lot of power in the previous phrases.

Everything starts with what you believe you are capable of. You may require a different approach for organizing your priorities and making them a reality without stressing out, burning out, or freaking out. Find what works for you. One thing is clear: We tend to focus on what is important and urgent. That means that we are reacting and not proactively planning to act on what is very important but not necessarily urgent. When you focus on the important-but-not-urgent tasks, you are working on activities that will make a difference in your long-term results and have the greatest ROTE.

SEVENTEENTH DAILY CHALLENGE

Review your PSC one more time and find your important-not-urgent priorities you will commit to over time. Follow the next tips to recognize important-but-not-urgent priorities:

- You must decide to act on them.
- They build skills, competencies, and new capabilities.
- They are focused on building and nurturing relationships.
- They require a balance between planning and executing.
- They produce the greatest results, and the ROTE invested is exponential.

Once you have them, select three to seven priorities. Later, make sure you create a plan to progress in little increments and follow through.

Examples of important-but-not-urgent priorities:

- "Train myself and work with a coach."
- "Learn how to delegate and train my team."
- "Create and execute my Personal Strategy Canvas™."
- "Spend quality time with my loved ones."
- "Create my budget and monitor it constantly."

- "Boost my soft skills and practice with others."
- "Ask for feedback and adjust my habits."

Your priorities will determine your reality. We all have the same twenty-four hours per day. You can decide how to use them to bring you the most value in the short, medium, and long term. Every second that passes is gone forever. It is about you mastering the art of your self-management.

Life unfolds on a great sheet called Time
and once finished is gone forever.

—Chinese adage

Step Ten: Daily Focus

The smallest of action is better than the greatest of intentions.

—Mohammed Imran Uddin

Your Daily Routine

Your daily routine is what differentiates your plans from your results. In order to achieve what you want, you must act on your highest priorities. People looking for the shortcut usually see success as something they "buy," like buying a house. That is not sustainable because that house will require maintenance, improvements, and many other efforts to make sure it is suitable for you to live in. Similarly, we should nurture our own success daily. We must pay our daily "fee" to make sure we have a continuous progress toward our vision. That fee is your daily routine.

In the first chapters, I shared Gonzalo's story in which he created a daily routine to finish an Ironman.

He did it by knowing exactly what he wanted to achieve, his motivations, and when he would accomplish it. Then he planned and executed with consistency at every step. Let's play a game together and imagine that you want to run a marathon but haven't exercised before. You start by asking yourself, *Is it possible?* Be mindful about your thoughts, because whatever you believe will impact what you feel, your goal-setting, and what you are capable of achieving. Imagine that you are certain that you can, so you start to build your plan:

- Who has done it before?
- Who can guide or train me?
- Who can coach me?
- Who can make my path easier and more enjoyable?
- What are those tiny steps of a stairway that I will build to get there?

Now imagine that you start walking a mile two days a week. Then you start jogging a mile three times per week during the next couple of weeks. Then you become more consistent and set a schedule for your trainings. Four days per week: Two days you jog, and the other two days you walk two miles. Then you feel good and start running two miles four days per week. Weeks later, you run five miles four days per week, and on the other days, you go to the gym. After some months, you will see you are feeling good. You are really making progress because you committed to a process of self-development that requires training and consistency over time.

Then imagine you become part of a group of runners, and you all train together. You are experiencing the joy of people guiding and inspiring you. With that kind of commitment, of course you will run your marathon! Does that work the same way for everybody? Not necessarily, because it depends on many factors, starting with how that goal is feeding your visionary mind (vision, purpose, and values). How is that goal tied to your inner motivations, and why do you want to accomplish it? For example, I personally do not enjoy running or swimming for hours, but I can be at a budo seminar for many days, just training, sleeping, and eating. The point here is to pursue what inspires you. Using a similar approach as the marathon example, you will be able to achieve all of your goals. Be honest with your level of commitment, because it will define your timing to achieve your results. Let's work on your plan!

Your PSC: 10. Daily Focus

Your daily actions come from your top priorities; the difference here is these are activities to focus on every day. These actions need constant execution to achieve your results. It will require time, so you will create a daily "bubble of silence," a peaceful place where you can focus and become one with what you are doing. During that time, let your body express and show the best you have without interruptions. Let your talents flourish. Enter a state of mind where you don't allow any distraction because you know it can neutralize the divine moment you are having with yourself and your activity.

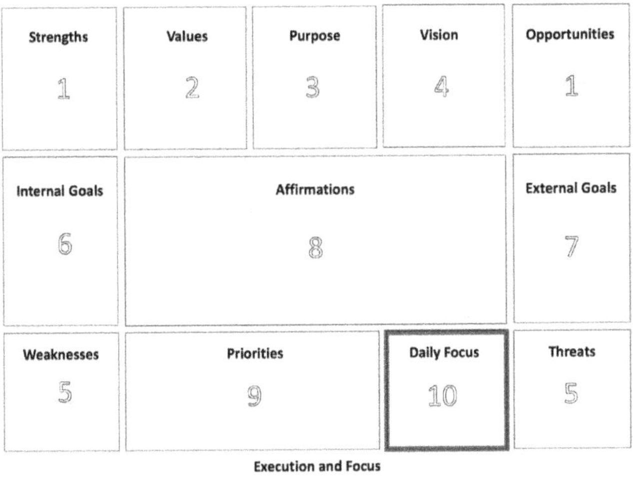

Strengths	Values	Purpose	Vision	Opportunities
1	2	3	4	1

Internal Goals	Affirmations			External Goals
6	8			7

Weaknesses	Priorities		Daily Focus	Threats
5	9		10	5

Execution and Focus

Figure 13: Daily Focus

Now imagine you are working on a project that will require approximately twenty-seven hours of your time. You know this because of your experience planning, practicing, and setting times. You know that with practice, you will be able do it in less time. You also know that you are not managing time; you are managing yourself. Therefore, you focus on disciplining your mind, your thoughts, and your actions. Your project must be done in six weeks, so you decide to work three days a week on it: Tuesdays, Wednesdays, and Fridays from 10:30 a.m. to 12:00 p.m. (perhaps after answering emails and finishing some urgent phone calls).

Then you put the timeslots in your calendar to make it visual. You will have it done in six weeks, because you are working 4.5 hours per week (4.5 hours x 6 weeks = 27 hours). With that plan, you will finish your project on time. You know the unexpected happens, so you schedule 1.5 extra hours on weeks two and four to create a cushion. Your contingency plan is three extra hours.

Of course, that's the ideal plan, and during execution, you may have to adjust. That's completely fine. Just find new slots to allocate the time. Of course, reality happens, and there may be some days that you will have to use that time slot, but instead of erasing that slot, you will move it to another place. Remember a time slot doesn't disappear. You are committed to making it happen, and you will move the pieces like a chess game. You are sure you will achieve it, so you work on it as planned. Every time, you shut down distractions and focus. The more you practice, the easier it will get.

How you set your daily focus activities is key because it must make sense across your whole PSC. Everything must be aligned in the direction of your vision, internal goals, and external goals.

EIGHTEENTH DAILY CHALLENGE

Write three daily focus activities, and make sure you don't overlap ideas in your canvas—the segments of your canvas must complement every other. At the end, that piece of paper will be your greatest tool for your success.

Use your preferred tool to keep track of your agenda and establish cyclic time slots (sixty to ninety minutes maximum) for each focus activity. Defend those times, and make sure to spend quality time on a daily basis. If something arises, move the time slot to another day; never erase it. Those are your highest priorities for your daily focus. Remember, what is not in your agenda does not exist.

Examples of daily focus activities:

- "Eat lunch with my family at 2 p.m. five times per week."
- "Call prospects from 10 a.m. to 11:30 a.m. Monday through Thursday."
- "Wake up and work out daily from 6:15 a.m. to 7:00 a.m."

Remember that in preparing for overcoming your challenges, your plan may be useless, but your planning is indispensable. It is pushing you to think and create new paths for your own definition of success. Your PSC is a living document. It will evolve. Remember to keep track of each new version. Be ready to adjust when any situation arises. One thing is certain: With discipline, focus, and perseverance, you will accomplish your goals, and every day, you will be closer to your dreams.

Congratulations! You just finished your Personal Strategy Canvas™. You have created the foundation of your continuous growth. Walk your path every day, and flow with it. The more you enjoy your present, the more you will be closer to your ideal future.

If you have continued reading up to here, you are doing an amazing job! I have three questions for you:

- Have you completed all the daily challenges?
- Did you finish your first version of your Personal Strategy Canvas™?
- Are you focusing your time and efforts on your highest priorities?

If you answered yes, congratulations! You are nailing it and are ready to continue reading about implementation, execution, and effectiveness.

If you answered no to one or more, it is fine. It is vital you enjoy your path. I know. It has happened to me that I continued reading a book and said, "I will do the exercise later." Scheduling is key!

Put in your calendar when you will complete tasks. Some of them will take just a few minutes, and some of them may take a few hours. Simply start and continue making progress.

Stop here and figure out how will you finish the challenges and when you will have your Personal Strategy Canvas™ ready to continue boosting your results. Let's do it!

Fall seven times, rise eight.

—Japanese proverb

Training, Perseverance, and *Mushin*

You can only fight the way you practice.

—Miyamoto Musashi, samurai and philosopher

When someone is good at a certain skill, usually the first thoughts that come to mind are things like "I wish I had that talent" or "They are so fortunate to have that talent." As economist and writer Geoff Colvin stated, talent is overrated—it is about deliberate practice.[10] There are many stories of "untalented" people who became known for what they do. Success is a question of discipline, practice, focus, concentration, repetition, and resilience. It is about the intention, the mindset, and the way you practice.

The focus should be not on talent but 100 percent on the process, on the training. We all can develop the skill, attitude, habit, and result we want if we focus on the way we practice, with patience and perseverance to get better. This powerful mindset shapes who we are. The way our brain is trained defines how we feel, behave, and grow. You can believe you are either good or bad at something, that you are talented at certain skills and not talented at others. Or you can believe you can get better at anything you choose and can develop any new talent, skill, or habit when you train over time with perseverance, focus, and resilience. The first is a fixed mindset, dependent on luck, natural talents, and destiny. The second approach is a growth mindset, dependent only on deciding where to focus time and effort to get better. Those with a growth mindset know there are no shortcuts, but that they will get better over time at absolutely anything they decide to focus on.

Have you heard people say they're not good at remembering names or learning a new language? I have also heard people say they're not good at selling, playing an instrument, dancing, sports—you name it. Sometimes they say they are great at one skill but not another, and when something is difficult, they just say, "I can't." Those people are expecting instant gratification. For example, they may expect to see results after training at the gym for a few weeks, and when they don't, they get disappointed and just quit. We have all been there, but every time you catch yourself thinking that way, just stop! We were trained to unconsciously think that way, because it is the easiest way to think. It is by far more difficult to take responsibility for our destiny, knowing that we are continuously growing. It is more challenging to believe that we are capable of everything when we decide to practice continuously. Once we achieve more of our results, our levels of responsibility increase, too. In other words, your own personal accountability grows.

Do yourself a favor and start believing that you can achieve anything you want when you commit to practice with patience, perseverance, and focus. If you continue thinking that you don't have the discipline or will to commit to that level of training for a particular skill—if that is truly the way you want to think—appreciate your self-honesty and make peace with yourself. It is very probable that skill is not a real priority for you. Probably, it is not serving your purpose. You may be motivated to do it because of social pressure or other external motivators. If you do believe that skill is an important priority in your life, then raise your self-awareness, change your focus, create your PSC, focus on your path, and train for your continuous improvement. You can adjust, you can improve, you can increase or decrease the pace, but you will never quit. Much more important than the plan is to find your inner motivation to achieve your goals. Continue your trainings with the only rule of continuing to move forward, and do not stop no matter what, especially when you believe you are not making progress. There is no perfect training plan— the value of your plan is that you are thinking about it and starting to create a system that works for you, for what is meaningful for you.

Make sure you continue on your path! Start slow and steady, then increase the speed and intensity as you make progress. When you start with little steps, you start building habits from the ground up. That way of thinking is the foundation of a growth mindset, the belief that we continuously evolve, that we can improve anything when we set our mind and actions to overcome it. A growth mindset means accepting yourself as a whole and as part of the universe, knowing that everything is possible. It is saying to yourself phrases like, "I want to get better at dancing, so I will take some lessons" instead of "I'm not good at dancing." It's saying, "I will get better over time" rather than "I can't." It is taking control of your growth processes, choosing your priorities, and living your purpose. It is knowing that when you decide to train and practice continuously, your mistakes will turn into your greatest teachers. Commit to living your personal Do for your self-growth.

Training and continuous practice over time will develop your skills in any way you choose. There are no shortcuts—just willingness to grow, get better, and consistently believe that you are capable of everything you choose to do. It is about believing in your own awesomeness, the awesomeness that many people around you know you have and many times you resist believing in. Having a growth mindset serves your life far better than having a fixed mindset. It has to do with embracing and committing to living the adventure of your own life. Put your ego aside. Make lots of mistakes, learn from them, and continue moving forward. That's the way a growth mindset makes peace with its own path, with its unique Do.

Continuously practicing what is meaningful for you creates new neural connections. You travel the path from an unconscious incompetence to a conscious incompetence to a conscious competence, and to, finally, an unconscious competence. In budo, we use a concept in Japanese to describe that last phase of unconscious competence, *mushin,* or "no-mind." Mushin is a state in which your brain is one with everything and you unconsciously act. You stop thinking. You are living the moment ready for the unexpected. We all have experienced mushin at a certain level. Think of times you were driving and then realized you just arrived where you were going. You couldn't remember how many green lights you crossed, how many turns you made, or even the route you took, in some cases. Perhaps in such moments, you sat in your car thinking about what just happened, even feeling scared because of the "mental lagoon," but it is nothing to fear. It is your brain performing a skill it has trained in for a long time—it already knows what to do and how to do it. Now imagine again driving on "autopilot" when suddenly a little kid crosses the street. You stop and avoid him, right away! Nothing happens. The kid is fine—that's mushin! You didn't think about pushing the brake or avoiding him. It was like a snap; there was no time to think. It can happen to someone while riding a bike, surfing, skating, or doing any activity they have practiced long enough to become part of their being. Mushin is to be here and everywhere at the same time, to be aware of your surroundings, to be in a place of contemplation and meditation where all your senses are alert. It all depends on what you have practiced over and over and over again. Mushin calls every cell of your body, and all of them know what to do.

Imagine you have just thirty minutes to finish a very important task for a life-or-death situation. You turn off your cellphone and any other distractions, close the door, and let someone know you will not be available for thirty minutes. You set your timer for twenty-five minutes, so you'll know when you have five minutes left. Because of that timeframe, you concentrate and focus your mind to have it done. You enter a meditation mode—mushin. It feels slow during the first few minutes, but then you ramp up and it feels good. You start wondering how much time you have but then let go of that idea and continue moving forward. Then you start reviewing your work, and it looks good. You are just focused on the priorities that must be included. You are saving your work and start to wrap up when the alarm rings. You are done and have five extra minutes for last details. It feels good. Training mushin can be one of your great allies while executing your priorities. It works by defining a time to finish a simple task. Historian and writer C. Northcote Parkinson introduced this concept as Parkinson's Law, which states that "work expands so as to fill the time available for its completion."[11] The less time available, the more you focus your efforts. In contrast, the more time you have, the more you will waste because you will use all the available time.

This is a simplistic explanation of mushin to share that we all have experienced it at a certain level. In budo, that no-mind is the difference between life or death, winning or losing a kumite. If mushin is there, you will be effective. In karate, the consequence will be a strong punch, kick, or a knockout. In iaido, the consequence of making a mistake is life or death. Another interesting aspect is that our opponent may also use mushin. While training, our best partner is the one who trains intensely with the intention that we will not have an enemy more dangerous or skilled than him. The intention of the practice is to perform as if in a life-or-death situation. Imagine you have an opponent with a sword in front of you, with a calm face because he also has been polishing his mind and spirit. You know a slight mistake will be lethal. The more you think about it, the more your mind interferes, and the more your mind interferes, the higher the probability of making a mistake. In a normal situation, we usually concentrate, think, and pay attention. But while training with mushin, we are at peace with death, with life, with winning or losing. We are at peace with any possibility. It requires a lot of training, and that's precisely the point I want to share. Any new skill requires focus, effort, and continuous training. It is not easy, but who said life is easy? Of course, it's not easy. That's precisely the beauty of life, the beauty of developing the skills to overcome any situation we face.

Every training requires your focus and consistent commitment to give your best, your ganbatte. Imagine that the achievement of your goals is a life-or-death situation. With that mindset, you will avoid any distractions. Make your trainings the most important aspect of your life to polish how you will achieve your goals. Your training process is as important as working on the tasks to achieve your results. Put all your spirit, mind, and body toward shaping what you want to develop. It is about experimenting, doing, and learning from the training. Traditionally in education, there has been too much emphasis on acquiring and learning big quantities of information. The main point is to learn and practice what is relevant for the achievement of your goals. Balance knowledge with execution, planning with doing, hard skills with soft skills. Make sure you are really taking the most advantage of your time training and practicing. Over time, it will let you achieve more with less time and effort. It will let you achieve incredible progress with the maximum ROTE.

The no-mind not-thinks no-thoughts about no-things.

—Gautama Buddha

Organizational *Do*

Spirit first, technique second.

—Gichin Funakoshi, *Karate-Do: My Way of Life*

We are living in very fast times. As explained in the book *Digital to the Core*, technology is taking over like a tsunami, we are already surfing the digital wave, and as individuals, we are achieving more in less time than past generations.[12] We are running, and the pace of life nowadays is so fast that if we are not careful, we may finish where we don't want to be. Because of that fast pace, we are forgetting to focus on ourselves and on connecting at a very profound level with others. Connections build relationships. Meaningful conversations make those bonds stronger, and those bonds are the seeds of our happiness. We are part of society—not from a country, religion, or gender, but of the world. As soon as we understand that we are here to help each other, we will be more capable of enjoying life.

We are imperfect, and we want to grow; likewise, our organization wants to grow, learn, and achieve a better state of well-being. Cash flow is a key part of the equation, but it is more than just numbers and financial achievements. It is about the organization's capacity to build relationships, to serve each other internally so that serving your clients is an incredible experience. It starts with you, whether you are an entry-level employee or the founder.

The organization has its own Do or path and is alive because of you and other collaborators. How you feel, think, behave, and act have a direct impact on it. When working with organizations in consulting projects, before we start, we make an organizational diagnosis. We analyze the business model, the operations, paperwork, and most importantly, we talk to people. We talk to as many collaborators of the organization as we can. They know what they share will be confidential. We ask many questions to uncover the root of their challenges at all levels of the organization, to have a systemic perspective on their challenges. We learn a lot from all of them. It is amazing that they already know how to solve most of their problems. It is just that no one has spent the time to ask those key questions and listen without any judgment. After asking all those questions, the common ground is clear, and we can explore where perspectives overlap. After all that conversation, there is a question we always ask:

Imagine you have a magic wand and could improve right away your biggest challenge. What would you change?

What keeps impressing me is that almost every time, they say they want to change something in another area, in other people. In a way, they say the solution is out of their reach. Very few times in fifteen years has someone told us, "I will change" or given an answer implying that. It is by far easier to see the solution outside, and it requires practice to see the solution from within. That's why our leadership programs create self-awareness in employees to naturally see that all the changes they want to see in others start with each of them. In our trainings, we use the common term "personal accountability," a key aspect to practice to progress in their self-mastery.

When you grow and you are part of the solution, many people around you grow. The inverse happens when you don't grow or get worse: The people around you regress. When that happens, the easiest route is to blame others. Years ago, a friend sent me a saying that goes something like this: "When you point fingers to blame others, you have at least three fingers pointing back at you." I say that means you must answer to yourself at least three times: What could you have done to avoid this situation? How will you fix it? How will you prevent it from happening again? By just stopping and taking responsibility, you will discover how many times you could do something differently as lessons for future situations. Remember, it is not about failing but about learning from any situation. It is your duty to work on your happiness and engagement in life—no one will do it for you. You are not alone. You will do it by training yourself and impacting the people around you.

If you are not growing, you are dying. If you don't use a skill, it atrophies. If you learn new skills and you practice continuously, you grow, and when you grow, your organization grows. Self-mastery is required to lead yourself first, and then you can inspire others. The same is true with your organization. Ask the following questions to determine whether your organization is growing:

- Who is leading?
- How does the leader promote communication?
- How does the chain of command work?
- How proficient are your leaders in leading their lives?
- How proficient are your leaders in leading others?

If you want your organization to transcend and have a happy journey, it is important to focus on three aspects:

1. How are you engaging in meaningful conversations (ones that go beyond operations)?
2. How are you using other perspectives (your openness to listen and use the information)?

3.   How are you improving from within (therefore your organization gets stronger)?

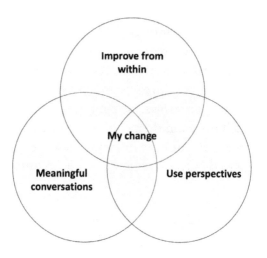

Figure 14: My Change

In a similar way that you are finding your path, your organization is finding its path, its truth, its own Do. When I see a karate class and how an organization interacts, I find so many intersections. Organizations can get better if their team members focus on honor, respect, camaraderie, justice, peace, collaboration, and discipline. An organization is not a *dojo*, but it could be, with its own authenticity and uniqueness. There are many books that talk about strategy, what shapes culture, how to build an organization that lasts, the right timing to achieve key milestones, financial success, and how to have an engaged workforce that performs to high standards. Yet we are whole people, living whole lives, learning and enjoying what is meaningful for us. We whole people decide, create, collaborate, and innovate in a way that nurtures each other to achieve a greater purpose.

The essence of an organization goes beyond the idea of performance and results, beyond collaborating like a family. The goal is to create value at all levels, to serve the people around us to benefit society and promote growth. Unfortunately, that is not always happening in some organizations. Growth requires humility, to put our ego outside of the equation to collaborate in any way possible and add value to the people we interact with. It is about knowing our values, the ones we use to make decisions, even the most difficult ones. It is about being consistent with who we are and finding a place to share who we are. We can even build that place for us and the people that share the same philosophy and spirit.

You have your own values, and your organization has its own values. Its values are determined by the way its collaborators behave and make decisions. That conjunction of values determines its organizational culture, its spirit. That gives the organization its own uniqueness, which can work for or against the organization. It depends on how intentional those values and culture are. It depends on how much each member of the organization understands who they are and how the organization explores its own identity over time. Like you, your organization is continuously changing, and therefore if all its collaborators feed it well and nurture its roots, its collective mind, body, emotions, and spirit, it will continue growing. Its longevity depends on all the people who make it work as a system. Everybody's contribution to creative collaboration sustains the organization and helps it achieve its purpose.

During the last few years, hierarchical levels have been vanishing within organizations. Even with that new structure, these organizations still work because communication flows at all levels, and people focus on what matters for the well-being of the organization. Its collaborators lead their own lives and choose to contribute.

All collaborators in an organization make a contribution, starting with giving their best as individuals. When each person lives their Do and applies their PSC, they are like a caterpillar transforming into a butterfly. Then when they flap their new "wings" of growth they cause a butterfly effect throughout the rest of the organization. The real power of personal accountability and self-mastery resides in the ripple effect caused by their daily attitudes and actions. When synchronized and aligned toward the same vision and goals, all those efforts multiply and expand. I am talking about synergy and how a team with a clear understanding of their individual and organizational Do can create a compound effect where exponential results are real. This same concept can be applied not only to organizations but to families, institutions, and countries.

Organizations are evolving because they are integrating new generations. We are learning to interact with and accept different points of view. We are learning that a person is not smarter because of the years working in the organization but because of the ideas shared with other people in the organization and their ability to solve situations in a dynamic way. The focus is on the solution rather than on who made a mistake or why a mistake happened. The trend of organizations is leading to a place where soft skills are more relevant than before. Organizations are understanding that not only are technical skills crucial, but soft skills are, too. Leaders in these organizations are not leading to look good or show off but to make sure people communicate effectively, ideas flourish, and results happen.

During the last few decades, corporations have been working like machines, focusing on goals, productivity, metrics, systems, more earnings, more work, and more shares, so the shareholders continue growing their investment. Other organizations perform under a new paradigm: They focus on the well-being of the organization and its members, not just as a family but as a single living being, with a strong purpose and values. Their clients experience a new level of commitment and service. These organizations focus on the human touch and make a difference because of that sensitive approach.

Start exploring a new way of thinking and a new way of delivering results. It must be with sympathy for others, caring for others, and responsibility for your own engagement. People in those organizations are happy not just for being part of it. They are happy because they are growing in the organization at all levels, not just as part of the workforce. They understand the importance of investing time and energy developing people skills in their workforce to increase their capacity to grow in all aspects of their lives. They know that by doing so, they are nurturing their culture to continuously grow stronger.

I believe an organization is a living being with many brains. An organization is alive, and I believe it also has a soul. This concept may disturb some people. Think about this:

1. What are the highest dreams of your organization?
2. How does it behave?
3. What does it like?
4. How is your organization feeling?
5. What are your organization's values?
6. What are your values?
7. How congruent are you with those values?

Finding those values and being congruent with them feeds the organization's spirit, gives meaning to its members, and makes them feel alive and proud of being part of the organization. Sometimes, an organization doesn't know its values or expresses its desired values rather than the real ones. When values are not clear or when there is no congruency, its collaborators feel regret, unhappiness, anxiety, and even sleeplessness. If you have been building an organization congruent with its values, you and your team can have sweet dreams because your soul is happy.

You may think you just work at your organization. I have some news: No matter how small or big your organization, you are a key part of it. What you do and how you behave is relevant. You certainly can make a difference from your unique standpoint. Your organization is alive: It feels, breathes, smells, and sees what's going on. Think about these questions:

1. What advice do you want to give yourself and/ or your organization?
2. What is your organization's purpose?
3. What will make its soul happy?

This concept is kind of surreal but very powerful if you are in touch with it. The purpose of your organization goes beyond sales, productivity, effectiveness, processes, and results. It doesn't matter your position in your organization. The question always comes back to you. To grow, it is vital you train and polish your leadership skills. Lead yourself and support others!

When the Way comes to an end, then change—
having changed, you pass through.

—I Ching

Modern Samurais

Mental bearing (calmness), not skill, is the sign of a matured samurai. A samurai therefore should neither be pompous nor arrogant.

—Tsukahara Bokuden, swordsman of the early Sengoku period (1500 AD)

The samurai spirit is still with us. As historian Hosoda Haruko said, "Those imbued with the samurai spirit are capable of serenely carrying out their work in the face of any adversity and have the willpower to master themselves."[13] Ancient samurai constantly faced life's essence by facing death with calm resolution, demonstrating their ultimate loyalty to whom they served. The samurai worked hard and endured intense training that made them both physically and mentally strong. They used that incredible strength for self-defense and to stand up for those who needed it, rather than intimidating others or acting upon them harshly.

Now imagine a modern samurai. As we use the ancient samurai virtues as an example, a role model, or a point of reference, we must do so with extreme respect and appreciation of the legacy, understanding that many of the virtues they developed came about during times of war.

A modern samurai can be any person committed to becoming a better version of themselves every single second, a person who is always looking for new ways to balance his hard skills (knowledge, experience, competences, tools) with his soft skills (emotional intelligence, assertive communication, accountability, motivation). A modern samurai's continuous growth serves all the people around them. This samurai uses the tools around him with the precision of a katana and is focused on living a memorable life on their path of self-mastery. A modern samurai is an honorable person with courage, willingness to sacrifice for others, and unremitting discipline. A modern samurai can be from any gender, age, race, social level, etc. They act congruent with their values and live with honor, justice, respect, and discipline. They are willing to go beyond their own accomplishments and ego to give their lives to create a better world.

Each modern samurai is unique and is part of an organization that relentlessly lives their values, their own code of conduct. Now imagine a world full of modern samurais who put honor first, taking care of each other and learning from each other. I know this concept will resonate with many people, while others might not feel sure of this idea. If the latter is happening to you, explore these ideas:

- What elements of this idea of the modern samurai do make sense to you?
- What is the right analogy for you to become your better self?
- How are you committing in your daily life?

Having trained karate for over thirty-five years, I have learned that growth and improvement comes from hours of practice, perseverance, and a mindset to continue, adjust, and never give up. It's all about having the humility to perform better no matter your level of skill. Therefore, growth is about giving your best to train your brain, body, and spirit every single day. Train and condition your well-being and teach it who is in charge. If the brain thinks about the right thing, just go and do it. A lot of times, we do what our body says, but if your being feels it is a good idea to wake up at 5:30 a.m. and run, just stand up and do it. If you know that there are important sales calls to do, just grab the phone and make them. Challenge your mind and your body. The least it needs is to be in comfort. The only way you will grow is by expanding your comfort zone. Everything starts with the right mindset, then the body follows. Your life requires your guidance and strong will to become the greatest person you can be. There are no shortcuts, but you can have nice surprises through your path, surprises that will make you feel that you are at the peak.

The opposite is also true. You can feel you are at the bottom of a situation. Or you might feel there is no hope, that life is unfair, and let's face it: Life is not fair or unfair; it's just life, and it can have the meaning you give it. Be authentic and accept who you are. When you are clear about yourself, when you are able to express out loud what you want, what you like, what you don't like, and still appreciate what you have, the world responds. People around you will notice it, especially when you are leading your own life toward the place that will make you proud, with the people you love, and with a smile on your face. You are creating and following your plans. You are passionate about it, and you are passionate about both sharing your points of view and respecting different perspectives. Your life is advancing in the direction you want. If you are going slow, it is OK; if you're going fast, it is OK. It's not a race. It's your trip, and you set the rules. You are a leader when you start leading your own life.

At the school where I practice iaido there are sequences of *katas* for each samurai value. To express each one of them is a challenge even though it may look simple. Each kata sequence requires many years of practice to be able to perform it at an adequate level. These are the values that the katas exemplify:

- *Meio* – Honor
- *Gi* – Justice

- *Ju* – Heroic Courage
- *Jin* – Compassion
- *Rei* – Respect, Etiquette, Courtesy
- *Makoto* – Absolute Sincerity
- *Chugio* – Loyalty

Gichin Funakoshi, the founder of shotokan karatedo, said, "In the past, it was expected that about three years were required to learn a single kata, and usually even an expert of considerable skill would only know three, or at most five, kata." In karatedo, I have been training sixteen katas throughout my life, and I am still far away from the level of skill that each kata requires. Something similar is happening in iaido, with the difference that at this point, I have been practicing more than thirty-five katas. Even though my skills are getting better year after year, I know I still have a long path in front of me and hope I have enough life to polish each one of them.

Practicing kata is very important in budo. It is a sequence of martial techniques created to practice with imaginary enemies, because it could be lethal to train it with partners with the right intention. I like how writer and practitioner of Japanese martial arts Kenji Tokitsu describes it: "a sequence of formalized and codified movements arising from a state of mind that is oriented toward the realization of Do (the way)."[14] Each kata has hidden secrets to be discovered during years of continuous practice. It takes a lifetime to polish each one. It is full of details and a great way to synchronize body, mind, and spirit. Each kata has to be performed with tranquility, speed, effectiveness, and precision. We practice with great discipline, as we cannot get it wrong. With practice, each technique becomes our second nature, to be expressed spontaneously when necessary. After many years of constant practice, our mushin is in charge, and we are constantly tightening our mind and spirit with kime. The goal is to do it without thinking. Our mind shouldn't be in a place but at the same time is completely present. It is meditation. It is mindfulness. It is polishing your whole being.

Like these kata sequences, any skill requires continuous development. It is a path that once started, never ends. I like thinking that when I wake up, I perform a long kata throughout the day. I spend the day looking for details to improve, self-awareness, how to be calm at all moments, and what I am learning from my mistakes. I believe each of our lives is a very long kata. We just have one life, and we should take the most advantage of it by getting better.

We are very complex creatures that are born, grow, and die. What happens in the process is 100 percent your responsibility. It doesn't matter if you were raised in a caring family, a conflicting family, or no family at all. People exist to excel in their lives by just accepting what they have and committing to what they want. It requires effort, learning the tools to succeed, and the willingness to take control of your life.

What if I told you there was a shortcut for your success, like a pill that helps you learn while you dream, exercise while you rest, improve while you do nothing, and change your life? What if I said the only thing you must do is to think about your dreams with all your heart, mind, body, and spirit, for long enough to make it appear in your life? That you must just have faith in it? It is important to know and believe in what you want, but it is also important to execute daily in creating your path. That's why the Personal Strategy Canvas™ is effective. Implementing it improves your life and the lives of the closest people around you. Some people say, "See to believe," but I believe it is exactly the opposite: "Believe to see" or intensely live your path to see. To lead, you don't need followers but must just progress in your self-mastery. When you are accountable for your present and your future, you are a leader because you are leading your own life.

Just as it is not appropriate to call ourselves a sensei but to allow the people around us to decide, something similar happens with many other titles. Recognitions are earned thorough effort. However, the goal is not to obtain recognition but to live a path pursuing self-mastery. That's precisely the core of this book, to be the living example of your essence. This book will not make you master the skills and concepts expressed in it, but it will raise your self-awareness about what you decide to practice continuously, to make it your path. A book, workshop, coach, or training are great tools to boost your talents. But if you limit yourself to that or believe that your participation in a program or a certification is showing your level of skill, you are mistaking it. You are the one who gives meaning to who you are. For example, a black belt can be bought by someone who became a black belt years ago but has long stopped working on their self-mastery. A black belt is just a piece of colored cloth around someone's waist, and it can be worn by anyone. The same happens with a certificate, diploma, or any recognition. These don't define you. What defines you are your actions and the meaning you give to each of those accomplishments. The goal is to get better day after day, to enjoy the process of continuous development, to give meaning to your life. A black belt is not even shown by the way someone kicks, blocks, and punches. It is shown by the way the person behaves and makes decisions in life. I really hope this book can ingrain in your soul the relevance of your continuous growth in all aspects of your life so you can serve better your society, add value to the world, and live your life with love and justice.

To all those whose progress remains hampered by ego-related distractions, let humility—the spiritual cornerstone upon which karate rests—serve to remind one to place virtue before vice, values before vanity, and principles before personalities.

—Sokon "Bushi" Matsumura, one of the original karate masters of Okinawa

Glossary

- AIKIDO ("eye-kih-doh") – Modern Japanese martial art developed by Morihei Ueshiba, also known as the way of unifying with life energy, or the way of peace and harmony. Aikido is an art that practitioners use to defend themselves while also protecting their attacker from injury.
- AIKIDOKA ("eye-kih-doh-ka") – Practitioner of the martial art aikido.
- ARIGATO GOZAIMASU ("a-ree-gah-toh goh-zah-ee-mah-suh) – Thank you.
- BOKKEN ("boh-kehn") – Japanese wooden sword used for training. It is usually the size and shape of a katana but is sometimes shaped like other swords. Bokken should not be confused with shinai, practice swords made of flexible bamboo.
- BUDO ("boo-doh") – Japanese martial arts. *Bu*, as translated in etymological definition, means "to stop a spear, and quell the violence." *Do* means the axiological essence of "the way." It implies suppression and control of violence by optimum force and reasoning based on justice. It also means

"martial way," meaning a warrior way of life devoted to self-development.

- BUDOKA ("boo-doh-ka") – Japanese martial arts practitioner.
- BUSHI ("boo-shee") – A warrior of the samurai caste.
- BUSHIDO ("boo-shee-doh") – The way of the warrior. Instructional code of conduct that dictated the samurai way of life. It was developed between the sixteenth and twentieth centuries but came into common usage after the 1899 publication of Inazo Nitobe's book *Bushido: The Soul of Japan*.
- CHIBURI ("shee-buh-ree") – Process by which one symbolically removes blood from a sword blade. It is translated as "shaking off the blood." In the Japanese martial art of iaido, this is done before nohtoh or placing the blade back into the scabbard.
- CHUGIO ("shuh-gih-oh") – Loyalty.
- DO ("doh") – Way, path, or truth. The Japanese character for Do is the same as the Chinese character for Tao (as in "Taoism"). It is intended to attain a state of natural peace and harmony through the path of personal quintessence.
- DOJO ("doh-ee-oh") – "Place of the way," also "place of enlightenment." The place where we practice Japanese martial arts, where personal Do is discovered. Traditional etiquette prescribes bowing in the direction of the designated front of the dojo whenever entering or leaving the dojo.

- GANBATTE ("gahn-bah-teh") – A polite and softer way of asking or telling someone to do their best or to not give up. It can probably be used with just about anyone, so long as they are not very superior to you. To be even more polite, you would add the word *kudasai* after *ganbatte*. "*Ganbatte kudasai*" can safely be used even with very senior people.
- GI ("gee") – Japanese martial arts uniform. Thus, a karategi means a karate uniform.
- HAKAMA ("hah-kah-mah") – Traditional Japanese trousers that are tied at the waist and fall approximately to the ankles. Nowadays, Japanese people wear hakama only on extremely formal occasions, like at tea ceremonies or weddings. Hakama are also regularly worn by practitioners of a variety of martial arts, such as iaido and aikido.
- IAIDO ("ee-eye-doh") – Japanese martial art that emphasizes being aware and capable of quickly drawing the sword and responding to a sudden attack; also known as the way of mental presence and immediate reaction. Iaido is associated with the smooth, controlled movements of drawing the sword from its scabbard, striking or cutting an opponent, removing blood from the blade, and then replacing the sword in the scabbard.
- IAITO ("ee-eye-toh") – Sword without sharpness, used primarily for practicing iaido.
- IKIGAI ("ee-kih-gah-ee") – A reason for being. It is used to indicate the source of value in one's life

or the things that make one's life worthwhile. It reflects the inner self of an individual and expresses that faithfully, while simultaneously creating a mental state in which the individual feels at ease. Activities that allow one to feel ikigai are often spontaneous and always undertaken willingly, giving the individual satisfaction and a sense of meaning to life.

- JIN ("jeen") – Compassion.
- JU ("juh") – Heroic courage.
- KADO ("kah-doh") – The way of flowers. Also known as ikebana, this art goes beyond simply taking a few flowers and artistically placing them in a pot. It encompasses a multiplicity of art forms, a study of relationships, and a key element of the Japanese character. Kado is a uniquely Japanese expression of contemplative beauty.
- KARATE ("kah-rah-teh") – "Empty hand." Modern martial art discipline and system of combat developed on Okinawa emphasizing blocking, striking, and kicking.
- KARATEDO ("kah-rah-teh-doh") – "The way of the empty hand." This implies not only the physical aspect of karate but also the mental and social aspects. Karatedo is a way of attaining enlightenment or a way of improving one's character through traditional training.
- KARATEGI ("kah-rah-teh-gee") – Karate uniform.
- KARATEKA ("kah-rah-teh-kah") – A practitioner of karate.

- KATA ("kah-tah") – A sequence of formalized and codified movements arising from a state of mind that is oriented toward the realization of Do or the path to enlightenment.
- KATANA ("kah-tah-nah") – Traditionally made Japanese sword used by the samurai of ancient and feudal Japan. Characterized by its distinctive appearance: a curved, single-edged blade with a circular or squared guard and long grip to accommodate two hands.
- KENSHI ("kehn-shee") – Swordsman. In iaido this title means "sword saint," and it is only given to the founder of a school.
- KI ("kee") – Mind, spirit, energy, vital force, intention. The definitions presented here are very general. *Ki* is one word that cannot be translated directly into any language. It also means "spirit," "breath," and "life force."
- KIAI ("kee-eye") – A shout from the gut delivered for focusing all of one's energy into a single movement. Even when audible "kiai" is absent, one should try to preserve the feeling of kiai at certain crucial points within budo techniques. It is also the manifestation of ki, a simultaneous union of spirit, and an expression of physical strength to concentrate life force into a spirit shout.
- KIME ("kee-meh") – Focus of power to tighten the mind or to focus body, mind, and spirit. Describes the instantaneous tensing at the correct moment during a technique. The tension at this time is

mostly focused on the abdomen as the energy center. In budo, the term refers to attacking a pressure point.

- KIOTSUKE ("kee-oh-tsuh-keh") – Attention. Stand with open hands down both sides.
- KIRITSUKE ("kee-ree-tsuh-keh") – Cutting; when the sword cuts through the air, practiced as one last breath of air and instantaneous flowing.
- KOKYU HO ("koh-kee-uh hoh") – Breathing done with the lower center of the stomach to slowly fill the entire being with ki energy. The sword must breathe together with the sword bearer.
- KUMITE ("kuh-mee-teh") – Sparring in martial arts, where camaraderie and respect are always present.
- MAKIWARA ("mah-kee-wah-rah") – Padded striking post used as a training tool in various styles of traditional karate. It is thought to be uniquely Okinawan in origin. The makiwara is used by karate practitioners to practice strikes in much the same way as a boxer uses a heavy bag. The makiwara develops one's striking ability by letting them experience resistance to punches, kicks, and other strikes.
- MAKOTO ("mah-koh-toh") – Absolute sincerity.
- MEIO ("meh-ee-oh") – Honor.
- MOKUSO (moh-kuh-soh) – Meditation to clear one's mind and to develop cognitive equanimity. Budo practice often begins or ends with a brief period of meditation. Meditation is an opportunity

to become aware of conditioned patterns of thought and behavior so that such patterns can be modified, eliminated, or more efficiently put to use.

- MOKUSO YAME ("moh-kuh-soh ee-jah-meh) – Stop meditation.
- MUSHIN ("moo-sheen") – No-mind. A state of being that allows freedom and flexibility to react and adapt to a given situation. Mushin is achieved when a person's mind is free from thoughts of anger, fear, or ego during combat or everyday life. There is an absence of discursive thought and judgment, so the person is totally free to act and react toward an opponent without hesitation and without disturbance from such thoughts.
- NOHTOH ("noh-toh") – Returning the sword to the scabbard.
- NUKITSUKE ("nuh-kee-tsuh-keh") – Sword drawing; practice of one silent breath of air and instantaneous departure.
- ONEGAI SHIMASU ("oh-neh-gah-ee shee-mah-suh") – To make a request or when asking. This is said while bowing to one's partner when initiating practice and to the instructor at the beginning of training; in that context, it could mean, "Teach me, please."
- OSS ("oh-ss") – The word *oss* is written as a two-character combination. The first character means "to push," and the second means "to suffer." Together they symbolize the importance of pushing, striving, and persevering while suffering through

whatever difficulties, pains, and hindrances are encountered along the way. It is a simple affirmation of the positive attitude, high spirits, and refusal to quit that all karatekas seek to develop as they train.

- REI ("reh-ee") – Respect. A method of showing respect in Japanese culture is the bow. It is proper for the junior person to bow lower than the senior person. Etiquette dictates that one should bow when entering the dojo or training area, when greeting the sensei, when greeting a black belt budoka, when beginning or ending a training session with a partner, when beginning or ending a kata performance, and when someone bows to one.

- RENSHI ("rehn-shee") – Renshi literally means "polished expert." This is the first level of the shogo or teaching-title system. In many organizations, this requires a minimum rank of yondan (fourth degree black belt).

- SADO ("sah-doh") – The way of tea. Japanese cultural activity involving the ceremonial preparation and presentation of powdered green tea. Zen Buddhism was a primary influence in the development of the Japanese tea ceremony. Preparing tea in this ceremony means pouring all one's attention into the predefined movements. The whole process is not about drinking tea but is about preparing a bowl of tea from one's heart.

- SATORI ("sah-toh-ree") – Japanese Buddhist term for awakening, comprehension, and understanding. It is commonly translated as "enlightenment."

- SAYA ("sah-yah") – Japanese sword scabbard.
- SAMURAI ("sah-moo-raee") – Literally "one who serves." A disciplined warrior in feudal Japan who led the military from the seventh to the nineteenth centuries. A member of the elite class in feudal Japan's four-caste (merchant, artisan, peasant, warrior) social order.
- SENPAI ("sehn-pah-ee") – A senior or advanced trusted student in the training hall.
- SENSEI ("sehn-seh-ee") – Teacher. Japanese term translated as "person born before another" or "one who comes before." The word is also used as a title to address other persons of authority or to show respect to someone who has achieved a certain level of mastery in an art form or some other skill.
- SHIHAN ("shee-hahn") – Master instructor, an example to follow.
- SHINKEN ("sheen-kehn") – Japanese sword that has a live forged blade. Literally meaning "live sword." The word is used in contrast with bokken or wooden sword. Shinken are often used in iaido for combat or cutting practice.
- SHODAN ("shoh-dahn") – First level, as in first-degree black belt. Literally meaning "beginning degree," it is the lowest black belt rank in Japanese martial arts. Nidan means second black belt rank, sandan is third black belt rank, yondan is fourth black belt rank, and so on.
- SHODO ("shoh-doh") – The art of calligraphy. Form of calligraphy, or artistic writing, of the

Japanese language. Shodo was influenced by Zen thought; for any particular piece of paper, the calligrapher has but one chance to create with the brush. The calligrapher must concentrate and be fluid in execution; even a lack of confidence shows up in the work. The brush writes a statement about the calligrapher at a moment in time. It is based on the principles of Zen Buddhism, which stresses a connection to the spiritual rather than the physical.

- ZEN ("zeh-n") – The Japanese meditative sect of Mahayana Buddhism. Zen emphasizes rigorous self-control, meditation practice, insight into the nature of things, and the personal expression of this insight in daily life, especially for the benefit of others.

Notes

1. Hyams, *Zen in the Martial Arts*, 11.
2. Hamada, *Quintessence of Japanese Classical Martial Arts*, 13.
3. Schwartz and McCarthy, "Manage Your Energy, Not Your Time," 2
4. Robbins, *The 5 Second Rule*, 175.
5. Nitobe, *Bushido*, 63.
6. Goldsmith, "Leadership Development: Try Feedforward Instead of Feedback," 15.
7. De Bono, *Six Thinking Hats*, 7.
8. Doran, "There's a S.M.A.R.T. Way to Write Management's Goals and Objectives," 35.
9. Hyams, *Zen in the Martial Arts*, 78.
10. Colvin, *Talent Is Overrated*, 17.
11. Parkinson, *Parkinson's Law*, 2.
12. Raskino and Waller, *Digital to the Core*, 83.
13. Haruko, "Samurai Spirit Still Animates Japan."
14. Tokitsu, *The Katas: The Meaning Behind the Movements*, 16.

Bibliography

Colvin, Geoff. *Talent Is Overrated*. New York: Penguin Random House, 2008.

De Bono, Edward. *Six Thinking Hats*. New York: Back Bay Books, 1999.

Doran, George T. "There's a S.M.A.R.T. Way to Write Management's Goals and Objectives," Temple University Fox School of Business Website, 1981. https://community.mis.temple.edu/mis0855002fall2015/files/2015/10/S.M.A.R.T-Way-Management-Review.pdf.

Goldsmith, Marshall. "Leadership Development: Try Feedforward Instead of Feedback," *Journal of Excellence*, Issue No. 8, 2003.

Hamada, Hiroyuki Tesshin. *Quintessence of Japanese Classical Martial Arts*. Dubuque Kendall/Hunt, 1990.

Haruko, Hosoda. "Samurai Spirit Still Animates Japan," Last modified December 6, 2011. www.nippon.com/en/column/g00009/.

Hyams, Joe. *Zen in the Martial Arts*. New York: Bantam Books, 1979.

Nitobe, Inazo. *Bushido*. Barcelona: Obelisco, 1989.

Parkinson, C. Northcote. *Parkinson's Law*. New York: Buccaneer Books, 1996.

Raskino, Mark, and Graham Waller. *Digital to the Core. New York:* Bibliomotion, 2015.

Robbins, Mel. *The 5 Second Rule*. New York: Savio Republic, 2017.

Schwartz, Tony, and Catherine McCarthy. "Manage Your Energy, Not Your Time." *Harvard Business Review*, October 2007.

Tokitsu, Kenji. *The Katas, The Meaning Behind the Movements*. Rochester: Inner Traditions, 2002.

Further Reading

Basho, Matsuo. *Narrow Road to the Interior*. Boston: Kodansha International, 1999.

Baynes, Wilhelm. *I Ching, The Ancient Chinese Book of Change*. New Jersey: Princeton University Press, 1950.

Bokuden, Tsukahara. *The Hundred Rules of War*. California: Createspace Independent Publishing Platform, 2017

Coquet, Michel. *Iaido, The Art of Cutting Ego*. Tours: Mystery Schools, 2016.

Deshimaru, Taisen. *Questions to a Zen Master*. New York: Arkana, 1991.

Draeger, Donn F. *Classical Budo*. Tokyo and New York: John Weatherhill, 1973.

Draeger, Donn F. *Classical Bujutsu*. Tokyo and New York: John Weatherhill, 1973.

Draeger, Donn F. *Modern Bujutsu & Budo*. Tokyo and New York: John Weatherhill, 1974.

Funakoshi, Gichin. *Karate-Do: My Way of Life*. Madrid: Eyras, 1986.

Kauz, Herman. *The Martial Spirit*. New York: The Overlook Press, 1977.

Kyokai, Bukkyo Dendo. *The Teaching of Buddha*. Tokyo: Kosaido Printing, 1966.

Miller, John G. *The Question Behind the Question*. New York: Penguin Putnam, 2001.

Morgan, Forrest E. *Living the Martial Way*. New Jersey: Barricade Books, 1992.

Musashi, Miyamoto. *The Book of Five Rings*. Denver: Shambhala Publications, 1998.

Nishiyama, Hidetaka, and Richard C. Brown. *Karate: The Art of Empty Hand Fighting*. Tokyo: Tuttle Company, 1959.

Random, Michael. *Japan: Strategy of the Unseen*. Madrid: Eyras, 1988.

Sunadomari, Kanshu. *Enlightenment through Aikido*. California: Blue Snake Books, 2004.

Turnbull, Stephen. *Samurai: The Story of Japan's Great Warriors*. New York: PRC, 2004.

Tzu, Lao. *Tao Te Ching*. New York: Columbia University Press, 1993.

Tzu, Sun. *The Art of War*. Mexico City: Tomo, 1998.

Ueshiba, Morihei. *The Art of Peace*. Boston: Shambhala Publications, 1969.

About the Author

Organizational Change Management

Genaro Torres is the founder of GTC Consulting, a leadership and change-management organization focused on talent management. He is a bicultural executive coach and business consultant collaborating with leaders in organizations in the United States and Latin America.

Genaro holds an MS in Systems Thinking Engineering and Planning, a BS in Industrial Engineering, and professional certifications from the International Coach Federation, the Center for Coaching Certification, and the University of San Diego.

He has taught at the San Diego Community College District, collaborated with the San Diego Organization Development Network, and is currently chair of the Association for Talent Development Mentorship Program. For his volunteer efforts, he earned the Distinguished Service Award from the American Society for Training and Development.

Japanese Martial Arts

Sensei Torres committed to the practice of karatedo (the art of the empty hand) when he was four years old in Mexico City at Casa Del Sol Dojo with Sensei Antonio Belmont and Sensei Juan Leonel Sierra in 1983. At the age of thirteen, Sensei Belmont recruited him as senpai, starting Torres's career as an assistant instructor in all classes.

He earned recognition in several tournaments, became a fourth-rank black belt in karatedo, became a first-rank black belt in iaido (the way of the sword), and continued to teach karatedo for the next twenty-five years.

He has been recognized with the title *Renshi* ("polished expert") by the International Seishinkai Karate Union and is an active member of Dai Nippon Butoku Sai, the most prestigious organization in traditional Japanese martial arts, based in Kyoto, Japan.

Sensei Torres has devoted his life to sharing the same gift that was given to him from his sensei—using karate to live with justice, camaraderie, respect, and honorability. In 2007, he opened a dojo in San Diego, where he enthusiastically shares his knowledge of karate and Japanese self-defense with students of all ages.

PERSONAL STRATEGY CANVAS

STRENGTHS	VALUES	PURPOSE	VISION	OPPORTUNITIES
List 3 to 7	List 3 to 7 unquestionable values	Describe your purpose in 8 words	Describe your future 5 years from now (35 words maximum)	List 3 to 7

INTERNAL GOALS	AFFIRMATIONS			EXTERNAL GOALS
List maximum 3 (attitudes / habits)	List a maximum of 10 positive statements in present tense to which you commit with yourself			List maximum 3 (projects)

WEAKNESSES	PRIORITIES	DAILY FOCUS		THREATS
List 3 to 7	List 3 to 7 key actions that will ensure the achievement of your goals	3 daily focus activities (90min)		List 3 to 7

CPSIA information can be obtained
at www.ICGtesting.com
Printed in the USA
FSHW021606011020
74352FS